ARRIVAL PRESS

LONDON

POETS

Edited

By

SUZY GOODALL

First published in Great Britain in 1995 by
ARRIVAL PRESS
1 - 2 Wainman Road, Woodston,
Peterborough, PE2 7BU

All Rights Reserved

Copyright Contributors 1995

HB ISBN 1 85786 380 1
SB ISBN 1 85786 385 2

Foreword

London Poets is a collection of verse that gives an insight into how local writers feel about the area in which they live. Among poems about the landscape and nature, nestle works about individuals, the community and their way of life.

I am sure that you will enjoy reading *London Poets*, and savour this poetic tour guide in the comfort of your own armchair.

Suzy Goodall
Editor

CONTENTS

City At Night	Helen Griffin	1
On Richmond Hill By Richmond Park	Patrick Redmond	1
The Rolling Stones Picnic	Molly Drinnan	2
The Cold, Cold Streets Of London Town	Den W Johnson	2
Untitled	John Bardsley	3
Winter In Walthamstow Market	Neil Fraser	4
The Antique Shop	Patrick McEwan	5
Sheltered Home	Donald Ward	6
Sutton	R Morris	6
The Wall	B Wallbridge	7
Barkers Bank	F Forbes-Pointer	8
Twickenham	Isabella Anderson	9
The Rise And Fall Of Canfield Gardens	Dennis Cohen	10
The Tradescant Church	Imogen Wooder	11
A Train Journey To London	Martin Norman	11
The Never Ending Day	John Fowler	12
London In The Fifties	H G Hutchin	13
My Road	Victoria Theedam	14
High Street	M O Brazier	15
London 1994/5	Diana Nicholson	16
Wintry Impressions	Susan Swain	17
On Cheshunt Marsh	E Reading	18
Hampstead	Hugh M Morris	19
London Borough Of Sutton	M Faulkner	19
North Cheam	Val Harriott	20
A Street In Chelsea	Aileen Wakeford	21
November Night In Beddington Park	Valerie Coleman	22
The Lord Of Winter	Rose Nicholson	22
The Eyes Of Guy	P Jones	23
We're Getting There!	Frank Henry	24
London Square	Ann Rutherford	25
Kings X (Shallow Seas)	Martin Lee-Stephenson	25

Counter Theatreland	Helen Vaux	26
London Spring 1988	Wendy Vidler	26
An Invitation To London	H Cox	27
Metropolis Madness	The Bard Of Euston	27
Return To London	Shirley Jones	28
Our Capital	M Barker	29
History Of London	Terry Croft	29
Ode To The Driver Of The W3	Chris Shirley Smith	30
The New Night Shift Manager	Simon Robson	31
London	Duncan Lavie	32
I Love London	Thelma Hynes	32
50 Years Remembered	V Deacon	33
Advice To A Foreign Tourist In London	Janice Fixter	34
Childhood Memories	Georgine Theobald	35
Many A Contrast	Judith Mudd	36
Silvertown	Mary Brown	37
A Winter's Morning In Chelsea	Jill Isaac	38
The Underground Song	Leslie Waterell	38
Highgate Past	P Burton	39
Friendship	T McGinley	40
Lovers Meet	Parveen Dharr	40
The Only Echo	Richard Pinchen	41
The Letter	Gilbert Sofeso	42
Seasons	Linda Holmes	43
The London Bus	Joan Manwaring	43
A Blinkered View Of London	E Flynn	44
Departure - Going Away	T E Lake	45
London's Gold	P Catchpole	46
Hampstead Fair	David Moir	46
Rooftops	Robert Ford	47
City Spires	P Young	48
London Butterflies	Jenny Linehan	48
The City Of London	C Payne	49
The Sleeper On The Bench	C M O'Connell	50

Get To Know Your Haringey	Joanne Chadwick	50
London's Alive	P W Jones	51
London Life	S Stuart	52
Metropolis	Brenda Soderberg	53
Moving To Kensington	Pauline Mills	54
Kensington Gardens	Lucy Ambrose	55
The Sleeping Man	Sharon Halsey	56
Helen At The Bus Stop	Kevin King	57
Hammersmith Reach	Michael Henry	57
Living In London	Claire Edwards	58
Our London	Colin Allsop	58
Action Replay	Hari J Elliott	59
London	C R Malcomson	59
I Wonder Who Lives In A House Like This	Traci Adams	60
London - Held To Ramsom	J Carlsen	61
Our Great London	Jill O'Donnell	62
Armistice Day	Rosy Jones	63
A View	Christine Licence	64
Hampstead Heath	Carol Wilkins	64
A Day In The Capital's Fairground	Donna Pitt	65
A Visit To London	B Archer	66
Sunset On Wimbledon Common	Andrew Weston-Webb	67
A Wintry London	Sheila Nicholls	67
The Shuttle	Monica Gurney	68
Big City	Rebecca Smith	69
Rugged Identities	Colin Nixon	69
London	H Penry	70
The Pavement Artist	Mary Spain	71
Frosty Midnight. Dulwich Woods	Mary Stella Ling	71
The Thames - Our Thames	Fredrick West	72
London	Adam Campbell	73
Ode To Walthamstow	Lillian Smart	74
The Tree	Wanda Hayman	75

A Cleaner's Farewell To London	Jerome David	76
Untitled	Andrew Ebrahim	76
A Dog's Tale	Norah Carter	77
A Spring Walk By The Tower Of London	John Christopher Cole	78
All Gigs Are Off	Chris Hardy	79
Waiting At The Bus Stop	Janine Holder	80
All Railways Lead To London	Rafael Kimberley-Bowen	81
Progress	Sheila Watkins	82
2010	R Redmond	83
Cardboard City	Charles E Watford	84
Hope	Henrietta Hersh	85
Ravensbury	Samantha Mardell	86
My Street	Linda Farrell	87
London	Philip Meikle	88
Twilight In Richmond	Hazel Turner	88
Sold For Building Plots	Jean M Eyre	89
The Last Train	Matthew Hersh	90
Stratford East	Robert S F Young	91
Fate And Fatality	Chris Hamlin	92
A Walk In The Woods	Diana M Lock	93
Old And Lonely	Lesley Wright	94
The Begger	Catherine Whitehouse	94
Islington	Karen Barnett	95
Wallington	E Dimmock	96
Another Spring	M J Peachey	97
Our Market	Diane Hallsworth	98
Early Morning Dippers	D J V Wright	99
Great Giants	Stephanie C Rondeau	100
While Contemplating London	Jane Finestone	101
Belmont Road, Uxbridge	Kathleen McGuinness	102
Sensuous Golders Hill	Peter Phillips	103
The Woman And The Dog	Virginia Rounding	104
Without You	Sheila Osborne	104
London's Lonely	Harold Rossney	105

Kensington Gardens - August 1965	Isobel M Malcolm	106
Good Morning Sutton	Penelope Guy	107
Yellow Buses	G A Place	107
Heaven In The Making?	Janeyne Powell	108
Ode To Sutton	Claire Williams	109
The Lost Pond	Bryan Clarke	110
Field End Road	A Whitehead	111
London Town?	Tracy Francis	112
Beloved City	Brenda Hargreaves	113
Kaleidoscope	Pearl Leeds	114
To The Rising Sun Lake	John Hibbert	114
Saturday Market	Katy Johnson	115
Windy Chingford!	R D Hiscoke	116
High On Parliament Hill	Agnes Stein	117
Harefield - Church Hill In The Spring	Susan Coldwell	118
Granpa's Cap	G Traveller	119
Capital City Of Great Britain	J Dimmer	120
London	Joan Yeadon	120
Between Times	Marion Green	121
Inspiration	Jo Lee	122
Untitled	Candice Armitage	122
Tranquillity	Lynda Treacher	123
London Life	T A Tinling	123
London	Jean English	124
Love Among The Ruins Of London	Muriel Grainger	125
Think Cinque	Sylvia Ward	126
Carshalton Ponds	Cheryl Morgan	126
Sutton Serenade	Anne Healey	127
Echoes Of The Past	Maggie Knight	128
Dagenham	Frederick Manning	129
Sunday Summer Afternoon	Christopher Cuninghame	129
A Poem About London Life	Margaret Irwin	130
Untitled	Marina MacLead	130
Camden Lock	P Hopkins	131

London Borough Of Sutton	P Howarth	132
New Thoughts On Old Lines	June Armstrong-Wright	133
Camden Town	George Tardios	134
Beddington . . . My Home	Sue Brotherwood	135
The Divisions Are Fine	Rona Topaz	136
Breaking Point	Ojeh	137
London Life	Malachi Hall	137
Self Contained	M W Donaghue	138
The Thames	Linda Yantolo	138
Home	A Edwards	139
London Pride	Carol Godfrey	139
London Impressions	Antoinette Marshall	140
Random Selection	John Manley	141
The Street Where I Live	Leonard E Tweed	142
London	Janet Larkin	143
London Town	Enid M Roberts	144
Sydenham Hill Woods	Margaret Jackman	145
Clouds Over London	John Rule	146
Twisting Oliver Twist	R Green	147
By Train To East Dulwich Station, London	Priscilla Noble	148
Which Life?	Isabel Tredinnick	149
Ebony	Nancy Shanks	150
Elbows Greased	Andrew Nice	150
On Doing Research Into Donkeys	Joanna Mackay	151
Crystal Palace	Martin Nathan	152
The Branches Of The Yew Tree	Keith Ayres	152
Urban Zoo	Michael Austin	153
Swiss Cottage Library	C H Wood	154
Kings Cross	John Gould	155
Hampstead Heath	Susan Crocker	156
London	Harry Fenton	157
London, A Life	Martin Connolly	158
Yiewsley	Marion Pinder	159
Untitled	L D Mellish	160
The Lure Of London	Margaret Robinson	161

Forget-U-Not	Adrian Vale	162
Rip The Sweet Chestnut Tree Of Wanstonia	L E Wirtz	163
Hayes End Romance	Ron Lamerton	164
Just Up My Street	Jasmine H Newing	165

CITY AT NIGHT

Soft grey pigeons, as seen nightly
Roosting on a window-sill
Gulls perched by the river lightly
Haunting back streets, quiet and still.

Trees with mist-like leaves of black
Wispy fronds seen 'neath a light
Spaced along the tramway track
Eerie in the dark of night.

Quiet and peace our senses steeping
Eyelids close and tired heads sag
Till hungry alley cats come leaping
Searching through a rubbish bag.

Distant sirens, boatmen's cries
In a goods yard whistles blow
The night impressions which arise
From a city's ebb and flow.

Helen Griffin

ON RICHMOND HILL BY RICHMOND PARK

On Richmond Hill two squirrels cling
To a leafless tree where blackbirds sing;
An old man shivers and hobbles by,
Wiping a tear from a March-wind eye.

The river seems, from the Terrace height,
A winding flow of surging might,
And in the park in graceful state
The deer form groups by the Richmond gate.

Patrick Redmond

THE ROLLING STONES PICNIC

If you go down to Richmond today
You'll be sure to see Jagger at play
      He picnics with yuppies
        and entertains puppies
Rolling Stones down the Hill I've heard say

Molly Drinnan

THE COLD, COLD STREETS OF LONDON TOWN

Why did it all go bad? The good life you once had.
You cannot think, Your head feels like a bunged up sink.
You must get some sleep. But there's nowhere warm to lay.
You look for more paper. To tie around your chest.
Tonight the wind will blow icy round your bed.

It has been a lousy day. You feel ill, and want to cry.
The thought comes to mind. It would be better if you
were to die.
Some, passers by. Look at you with scorn in their eyes.
Some, in pity stop. To place a few pence in your hand.
Thank you Sir. Thank you Ma'am.

So cold. So cold. You mutter through clenched teeth.
As into a coma you gently slip. Slowly sinking to the
ground.
You wonder why all around is warm and bright.
Paradise. You start to cry. And with relief you sigh.
Here you want to stay. Oh no. It's fading away.
It is getting cold and dark again. Oh the pain.
Then a voice you hear. 'Into the ambulance with him
quick. We might just save him yet.'
What for. What for, you try to yell.
I have had enough of hell. Let me die . . .

Den W Johnson

UNTITLED

It's quiet in city streets tonight, and dark,
With leaden sky scarce showing a single star:
As quiet and dark as once long years ago
When muffled watchman carrying smoky lamp
Stamped his slow way along the muddy path,
Crying out to show he did his task,
'It's six of the clock, and a fine November morn.'

But day's not yet, and still the city sleeps,
A deep untroubled sleep, of mind at peace,
Though body's torn and wracked.
Against the lowering clouds are faintly seen
The grisly bones that once were clothed with stone
And housed a myriad souls at daily work;
Gaunt walls and empty steeples, once hallowed shrines;
Now silent tower of Bow, the massive dome
Of Wren's immortal temple, once ringed with flame
That threatened to engulf the world,
Now standing darkly, almost alone.

But silence, seeming of the tomb, grows less
And faint is heard, hardly perceptible,
The distant murmur of a waking world.
And slowly pales the Eastern sky
As a new day's sun
Strives to break the darkness of the night;
And suddenly against still sombre sky
Is seen outlined in fire
The emblem still of life in a desolate world,
Paul's mighty golden Cross.

John Bardsley

WINTER IN WALTHAMSTOW MARKET

Grey as an archive photograph,
Puddles lit by stall lamps
Disperse and reform,
As the feet of glassy eyed shoppers
March from one bargain to another.

'Get your summer clothes early!'
The smell of seafood and vegetables permeates the air
As the mulch on the pavement becomes a soup.
'Warm yourself up with a snack and a hot drink!'
The shoppers become more frantic as the stalls begin to close.

'No, love, you won't find it cheaper.'
'Yes, love, it's top quality material.'
'Buy it now, it'll be gone tomorrow.'
Under a storm cloud canopy
These voices drown out the rain.

Pushchairs crack the back of ankles,
Umbrellas gouge unwary eyes,
Muffled curses escape from woolly scarves,
And the vaporous breath of the stall holders
Seems full of unreliable promises.

Neil Fraser

THE ANTIQUE SHOP

Standing in the shop so bold
Selling furniture so very old
Paintings, a desk, an old armchair
Very old pots of earthenware.

On a shelf stands an old brass clock
Under which shelves are choc-a-block
Hanging from a wall is a tapestry of satin
Inscribed upon which are words of Latin.

Standing by the wall - serene in pairs
Are four very fine Queen Anne chairs
Passing time has not yet killed
These precious objects, made by hands so skilled.

For all these things were made to last
The present here lies in the past
Listen now to the brass clock's chimes
Heard before in olden times.

Lord or earl may have heard its call
As it stood so proud in some stately hall
No more now can they hear it call the hour
For rising now is past their power.

Musing on these things for a while I stop
For a quiet look in the antique shop
Musing thus I enjoy my stay
And gaze at this - our yesterday.

Patrick McEwan

SHELTERED HOME

Is it strange, this questioning,
this pause, this honesty?
Is it cleansing us now?
This earth, this universe
is all we know - and do not know
beyond the tenderest limits
of experience:
this street, this *home* -
this sheltered place -
the friends we live with, and the friends
who've gone . . .
until even the *present* forgets it still exists
- is grown too old to hear those echoes of
the past that's past, yet
cannot *quite* forget, wrapped in the love
of those who love us most.

Donald Ward

SUTTON

The streets of terraced houses, roads of semi-detached
From whence folk in their thousands are to town daily despatched.
From avenues of lovely trees, grass verges, pleasant parks
Bright stalls, boutiques and large shops like Woolworth's, Allders, 'Marks'.
There's Worcester Park and Wallington, Belmont Hackbridge and Cheam
St Heliers, Rose Hill, Carshalton, all places to be seen.
Then when at night the folk return in crowded bus and train
In fog and snow or sunshine, in drizzle and in rain.
Of those great London suburbs, Sutton Borough is the thing.
It's a good place to come back to, best of that outer ring.

R Morris

THE WALL

'They are pulling down the Wall' said the woman on the bus.
'What China's Wall?' said he.
No, the Arsenal Wall, that's stood for years.
Built by men with sweat and tears.
Each brick bedded in hopeless fears.
And man's inhumanity.

'They are pulling down the Wall' said the man in the car
'What Hadrian's Wall?' I said,
No! The Wall that was built by the men who died.
In the festering hulks by the river side
Who good British justice had caught and tried
For stealing a loaf of bread.

'They are pulling down the Wall' said the man on the bike.
'What the Berlin Wall?' said I.
No! the Wall where my Dad built the great big guns.
That killed the Turks, the Zulus, and the Huns.
And turned out bullets by tons and tons.
To blow the world sky high.

'They are pulling down the Wall' said the man in the street,
'It's the Arsenal Wall,' said I.
And brick by brick it will turn to dust.
The guns and machinery be left to rest,
Till all that's left is Wellington's bust,
And the river slipping by.

B Wallbridge

BARKERS BANK

Greenwich Park is a doggies' bank,
That will always take a payment.
Made at any time of day
On grass, or on the pavement.

Deposits are left everywhere,
For communal distribution.
By young and old, rich or poor
We all take retribution.

Profits gained upon our shoes,
Are taken to the car,
Unknown at first, but evident
Before we've gone too far!

Then ritual disembarkation
To skate round on the grass,
Peering hard at soles of shoes,
Not a trace must pass.

Even by Wolfe's statue,
In the semi-dark
Some saucy hound has marked
The spot, to view the Cutty Sark.

On Sunday, owners put their
Pooches through their paces,
And later, while the band plays on
We see some newer faeces.

Why we other folk are forced
To have this mess
Left by thoughtless pet owners
I can never guess.

One solution perhaps, would be
To swoop down like a hawk
Upon the doggies trotting by,
And whack in a big *cork* . . .

F Forbes-Pointer

TWICKENHAM

'Twickers' is well known for its
Rugby Stadium where crowds flock
to see the game.
Kings, Queens, Presidents, Old Boys,
Young boys eat hot dogs on the way.
the music starts the game begins
and the cheering lasts till the
best team wins.
There is another side to
Twickenham a peaceful pleasant
town you can take a walk
down by the river feed the
ducks or laze around, it's
full of historical places that
you'd like to go and see
and is a bus journey
away from Richmond and London
and more and more history.

Isabella Anderson

THE RISE AND FALL OF CANFIELD GARDENS

Oh no! They're here again!
With their diggers and tippers,
Their shovels and picks
Up to their old tricks.
Hammering and punching drilling and crunching
Lifting and laying, stacking and splaying
Spreading; raking; tarring and setting.

Here again with their road signs and cordons
Bollards and barriers - 'No Parking', 'Footpaths blocked.'

Yes they're here in force again
With petrol smells and diesel fumes
With their rat-a-tatting on their pneumatic drills.
They're here to bang and they're here to break
They're here to lift and then to scrape.
Here for trenching, deep and shallow,
Trenching wide and trenching narrow.

Here again! Yes.
With thin pipes; fat pipes, plastic pipes and lead pipes.
Straight pipes curved pipes, with pipes to push and pull.
With red pipes; blue pipes, with pipes of lurid green
With coloured pipes of every conceivable hue.

Oh yes. They're certainly here again. But who!
Gas men; Water men; TV Cable or Brit Telecom men?
I'm trying to guess why again. Are you?
... Surely some officials, have cunningly devised
A place for these men, to train and exercise!
For all those dedicated to 'digging-up' and 'filling in' again!
We acknowledge the need, but it's hard to give pardons,
To those suspected officials, who chose . . . Canfield Gardens.

Dennis Cohen

THE TRADESCANT CHURCH

The door opens to the garden
Where I had paused in paving stones and lunch breaks,
In the dreamy quiet of the London day
The essence of non activity
There. The garden continues to grow, regardless of my absence,
Ignorant of my presence. I walk in the paths,
And creation continues around me
In the timeless recollection of that which has hardly gone,
In the embroidery of the colours in the trees, in the blending
Of the fruits and buds, in the lacework of the paths.
The trees are richer now, the leaves profuse,
The flowers uncurl and berries bright.
All manner of silences the garden enfolds,
The silence of questions.

Imogen Wooder

A TRAIN JOURNEY TO LONDON

Swirling and churling,
Grey waters journey on,
Gentle meandering,
Tranquil wanderings,
Furrowing through willow,
Amid bleak winter green,
Mellowing stark order,
With creative twists and turns,
Streams so narrow,
Yet full of living water,
Passing so quick,
These scenes linger on,
No infringement from man,
As we speed on!

Martin Norman

THE NEVER ENDING DAY

Take almost any subject
you choose to write in rhyme,
you sometimes get just lost for words
and then run out of time.
Until you think of London Town
and life within that City
then words just flow, and away you go -
another lengthy ditty.
Life's never dull in London Town
the night life is supreme
with pubs and clubs and cinemas
no time to sit and dream.
Theatre-goers come to town
by bus and car and train
and when the show is over
they don't go home again;
not straight away, I mean, at least
they may go for a bite;
the restaurants are hundred-fold:
stay open late at night.
If your appetite's not good
you may prefer a drink;
again the scores of pubs around
are closer than you think.
If you're young and have the puff
to dance the night away,
why not visit Clubland
before tomorrow comes today.
If, after this, you're still awake
you could stroll in the rain;
then wait until the sun comes up
and start it all again.

John Fowler

LONDON IN THE FIFTIES

I remember London town,
Worked there didn't I, years ago,
First job junior clerk in Victoria Street,
Little firm so friendly, with the old fashioned lift,
Looking in the cabinets for that elusive file,
Going down to Slater's for their best Lyons coffee,
All the lovely perfumed girls, standing in a row,
At the Army and Navy Stores, where all is aglow.

I remember Hovis Mills, down by Vauxhall Bridge,
Little brown loaves, sending onto bakers' shops,
Here and there and everywhere, were sent the tiny loaves,
Invoice typists merrily, typing their long winding sheets,
Joe and Jack the storemen, having a little chat,
One in three, Saturdays, I had to work,
Mr Veal the Commissionaire, standing by the door,
Poor Mr Dagwood with his 555 State Express, cigarettes,
Later collapsing with a heart attack on the boardroom floor.

Working for the War Office next,
Typing at the Citadel, all covered with ivy green,
Doing the night shift, down in those deep yellow caverns,
Where Churchill had his headquarters, near by, not so long ago,
Typing through till midnight, then a little sleep, woken up at 3 am,
Just a little peep, then new Maxwell House coffee brought round,
Yawning slowly, stretching our tired limbs back to confidential news.

At last the clock shows seven, and it's time to go home,
Walking across St James' Park in the early morning dew,
Back home to Cheam, across another zone.

H G Hutchin

MY ROAD

My road on a council estate
Has changed character
As it is today.
Many have bought council
Houses
Which has added different
Appearances.
These houses have changed
In many a way.

Different porch fronts
Pebble dash on walls.
Extensions to houses
Larger grandeur not small.

House front gardens
Crazy paving
Garages on their side.
Leaded decorative windows
For somewhere they reside.

Walls built round houses
Red brick plain to see
One with yellow decorative
Impressive to me.

But as houses have
Changed
I am still glad to see.
Its character of friendliness
By its people is prominent
More special you'll agree.

Victoria Theedam

HIGH STREET

Suburbia.
The High Street.
The boarded-up shops
Where no-one ever stops
Except to look at the violent covered billboards,
Graffiti hiding the derelict shops
Amongst the brightly lit stores
That loudly proclaim their wares.
Sale! Sale! Sale!
Bargains for all!
Last few days!
Bargains this way!

Shuffling feet around the department store.
Bargains if you've cash to spare.
Bargains if you've not.
Credit cards,
Interest free.
Stop here, stop here,
The High Street,
Suburbia.

M O Brazier

LONDON 1994/5

It's winter time in London
The coldest season of the year
There's talk of central heating
Log fires and Christmas cheer
But down in cardboard city
Where warm breath mists the air
There's little hint of pleasure
Even less of seasonal fare.
The soup run may come daily
To reach the lucky few
While others rest in church crypts
Or stretched along a pew.
We pretend to show compassion
When hearing of their plight
Yet wear the latest fashion
And go home to bed at night.
Some fifty years have passed now
Since the end of World War Two
And if you'd been a Londoner
You may have joined them too.
So thank you lucky stars
When Peace we celebrate
Stop carping it's just history
When for some it came too late.

Diana Nicholson

WINTRY IMPRESSIONS

Dark at dawn
Drear at dusk
Vibrant and soulful,
Only those who busk.
Underground trains spewing out crowds,
Traffic and sirens - intrusive and loud.
Theatre and cultural treasures galore,
A class-conscious people who strive to ignore
Anonymous bundles on uncaring streets,
The crowds at the Palace, the Royals to greet.

A statue, a square, and hundreds of birds -
They're fed for the photos, their cries go unheard.
Strolls through the green lungs of Hyde Park and Regent's,
Echoes of orchestras, strident and recent.
Odd smells and strange sounds, London Zoo is in sight
We giggle and ogle, not pitying their plight.

Exploring museums and shopping at Harrods,
At St Paul's and Big Ben, the tourists are gathered.
The hustle, the bustle is all so exciting,
Living within it - a lot less inviting.
As one of the busiest cities, it's known
Amid so many people, why so many alone?

Susan Swain

ON CHESHUNT MARSH

As o'er the marsh I wander
In summer's hazy noon
When mists are veiling yonder
And wild flowers bloom
The grasses wave and shiver
Stirred by a rustling breeze
And all the heat's a-quiver
And dancing on the leas

The river gently flowing
Glides onward to the lock
The youths so idly rowing
Where floats the waving dock
And there the houseboats lying
So trim and neat to see
And burdened barges plying
Their slow path to the sea

The cattle softly lowing
How peacefully they stand
The patient fishers throwing
Their lines, from off the strand
And there beyond the sedges
The Abbey, tall serene
Through many passing ages
Has gazed upon this scene

My peace is like the river
That flows to meet the tide
By still and quiet waters
The Lord my steps doth guide
And I will follow ever
The path where He doth lead
For He'll forsake me never
He is my Lord indeed.

E Reading

HAMPSTEAD

Slumber nearest to the clouds, the rhymester said
When work is done in City and Whitehall.
The stars of Hampstead vault just overhead
Down the many ways from Christchurch, see nightness fall.
Time traveller climbed the stairs in the Royal Free
He saw Hampstead lapping down on every hill;
He fancied ten hundred years of history
Had painted in the lanes and paths, at will.
London oppressed time traveller, gentle Hampstead out of sight
Camden Town engulfed his spirit and his song.
Then glimpses of far Hampstead's meadows against the light
Time knew that he had journeyed on too long.
He took the rising roads to where minds and the airs go free,
To the woods and hills, the busy slopes, to rest in lovely North West Three.

Hugh M Morris

LONDON BOROUGH OF SUTTON

Borough bright with borrowed light
   hangs on the skirts of Blighty,
But at night,
   Rises in her dark mantle,
   Phoenix of Time and Style
    wraps her plumes of purple,
   Mile on Mile,
     Around her peacock shoulder.

M Faulkner

NORTH CHEAM

I have lived and worked here for nine good years,
North Cheam, I've watched as it's old face is ever changing.
The old hospital was pulled down, in its place new housing appears.
They have built a whole new road with nice houses at the back of
                                                        Marlow Drive.
The London Transport site became the centre of a huge row,
Who would buy and what would they build? We didn't want it to happen.
Our old Sainsbury's was ok, but on the LT site a new one stands now.
Their park became a vandal's paradise, graffiti, burnt benches and the like,
Where once the climbing frame, swings and rocking toys once stood
There is a bare fenced-off square, the children's fun had to be taken away.
Why can't those hooligans see that all this was for their own good?
Schools and shops here are still the best a small place can offer,
For most, the people are friendly and always pass the time of day.
We always help each other in our Avenue, we all have a useful
                                                        trade to share,
Some are plumbers, carpenters or mechanics, each has a special
                                                            part to play.
I wish others would follow our little community and all live in harmony.
We have a swimming pool and lots of churches, doctors and dentists too,
Vets and florists, social clubs, pubs, parks and playgroups.
With all this and more to offer, we extend a friendly hand of
                                                        welcome to you.
Come by and see us on your way to Epsom or Kingston, or even
                                                           to the coast,
I am sure you will be very impressed, you can reach us by bus or car.
Once you have driven through Morden, you surely cannot miss us,
But if you do, ask anyone you see and they will tell you where you are.
North Cheam, changing place, sought after area, *my home*.

Val Harriott

A STREET IN CHELSEA

At one end a river
The other a shopping centre
Lofty mansions line the road
Which once saw carriages and pairs
Now the street's a thoroughfare
Ceaseless noise, taxis, lorries, buses
In endless procession.
The quiet mews, where peace is bought,
Stabled horses, replaced by cars
Brightly painted doors
Match flowers in window boxes.
Monday, dustbin day,
And stench of rotten cabbages
Residents complain
Rates go up
Neighbourhood goes down.
I would not live elsewhere
For Chelsea is renowned
A famous artists' centre.

Aileen Wakeford

NOVEMBER NIGHT IN BEDDINGTON PARK

From suburban lit streets, into the dark
Of a November night in Beddington Park.
The mist coiled and wreathed
Over grassland and river.
Through dead autumn branches
Where leaves didn't quiver.
The paths so familiar during the day
Were treacherous and alien, with scent of decay.
The fog-muffled night veiled sight and sound.
When three silent swans appeared through the gloom,
Like estranged spirits, portenders of doom.
My senses alert, imagination aspark
I rapidly retreated from Beddington Park.

Valerie Coleman

THE LORD OF WINTER

White clouds are my trusted steeds,
As I ride on the back of the wind,
Lightning is my servant,
Thunder my command,
Snow is my long white flowing cloak,
That I spread when the light is dimmed.
Hail is the perspiration from my steed
And the reins that I hold in my hands.
I can make the waves from the sea rise high,
Then calm them down again,
Or darken the skies with my frown, and turn it blue
When I smile again,
As I travel around the world,
All the people are my herd.
I am the Lord of Winter
My voice will surely be heard.

Rose Nicholson

THE EYES OF GUY

Of you I know so little
As to me you cannot speak,
The time I see you is so short,
Only once a week.

I want to know your story
And all that it contains,
Your likes your needs,
All your fears and pains.

Allegiance you display
For all around to see,
What is hidden deep inside
That holds you back from me.

If eyes contained the written word
Your secrets I could reap,
In those pools so dark and yearning
Only you shall keep.

When I peer into your soul
I see a much loved friend,
He is missed so very much
His life came to an end.

With every passing glance
Your eyes speak out his name,
In you, dear Guy,
His memory I retain.

When I can touch and hold you
As your story is untied,
Maybe then, and only then,
I'll accept my darling died.

P Jones

WE'RE GETTING THERE!

Isn't it great!
The train leaves at eight.
In town before nine
In comfort and style
Over many a mile -
No need to panic or pine!

The coach takes much longer
Even from Ongar.
So avoid all the pain,
Let the train take the strain!

Does this sound familiar?
Or is it plain sillier
To trust all these words
That are just for the birds?

Train's not on time -
Leaves on the line.
Wrong kind of snow.
I don't want to know!
Points frozen again.
Let the *train* take the strain?

Frank Henry

LONDON SQUARE

Stately pillared houses stand in line around the Square
Where rosy blossoms shyly blush in corner beds,
The breath of starlings' wings disturbs the heavy air
And the towering oak tree bows its shady head.

Leafy patterns dance upon the wandering path
Between the wooden seats where sit the young and old,
The lovers pledge devotion they know can never last,
The aged watch with empty eyes their memories grow cold.

There are shadows of the long dead who once lived in the Square
Whose memory is stitched in gilded plaque upon the walls
Fleeting reminders of the people who once lived and perished there
In the shuttered buildings beyond the great arched doors.

Ancient oak, if you had but the power of speech to give
A substance to those figures that dwell within the mind,
Could tell us tales of the forgotten ones and of the days they lived
Within the Square, now silent, that all have left behind.

Ann Rutherford

KINGS X (SHALLOW SEAS)

Wave goodbye
Another dawn breaks on a perfect day,
As we pack the tools,
Of our trade away,
As the hours tick into sunlight,
The wind bites.
And I wonder if the words we speak,
Are just shallow seas.

Martin Lee-Stephenson

COUNTER THEATRELAND

He sat amongst the crowd that day,
His face was white, his lips were grey,
Upon his feet his home - a bag,
Around his form was swathed a rag.

His sole companion was the rain
That swept the warmth from where he'd lain,
And with it mingled a tide of tears
To spill his heart full of silent fears.

About him were those who did not perceive,
Listen, look or even believe
That he was there, a sign to show
How life can fail, how death can grow.

He didn't move or he didn't try,
Though perhaps to sleep or even cry,
He may have raised that fragile frame,
But now dead was the man who had no name.

Helen Vaux

LONDON SPRING 1988

London: bastion of brick-built flats and towers,
Old town houses, shops and streets of concrete grey;
Suddenly your drabness has blossomed in spring flowers -
Green leaves and snowy blossom breathe
the miracle of May.

Wendy Vidler

AN INVITATION TO LONDON

If you would like to visit us,
yearn to ride on a London bus,
see our royal stately places,
go to the classy country horse races,
taste a real english tea
scones, cream and jam, mmm lovely.
we'd love you to come, just book your plane,
we just can't promise it will not rain.

H Cox

METROPOLIS MADNESS

Oh to be woken by the early birds' trill,
instead of the noise of the pneumatic drill,
the urban blight of noise and traffic fumes
are really no match for peacock's plumes.

In town the space and room are in short supply,
people push and shove just to get by,
open fields and fresh greenery
is a better place for you and me.

Parent birds work hard to fill a fledgling's beak,
in town you can shop seven days a week,
fast food and take-away are a real eyesore,
litter-free streets we will see no more.

Police cars wail and dash through a city street,
the countryside silence is hard to beat,
to pass the time of day in a sincere way,
is much nicer than 'morning' or 'hey'.

Perhaps the time has come to stop and reflect,
about friendships we tend to neglect.

The Bard Of Euston

RETURN TO LONDON

April in Paris,
a walk by the Seine.
Summer in Rome,
again and again.
The Rhine in Autumn
to the eye is splendid.
Austria in winter,
its scenery remembered.

Now London by day and city by night.
All year round is a wonderful sight.
Nowhere compares to this vibrant place,
home to a people of multiple race.
The river meanders, its banks to delight.
A Tower, a Bridge - whilst Big Ben strikes.
embankment dwellers rise at dawn,
to mingle with tourists - a coin is thrown.

To travel afar by air, ship and bus.
Is good for the soul of some of us.
But here in Old London,
with spires parks and byways,
It's good to back,
at least that's what I say!

Shirley Jones

OUR CAPITAL

London! London! The name has a ring.
A name to make you sing.
Sing its praises loud and clear
The one place, we all hold dear

There's the Queen at Buckingham Palace
(Look hard you may see Alice)
Hyde Park, The Tower, and Zoo
Westminster Abbey and Big Ben too.

Buildings old, buildings new.
Such a lot of things to do .
Feed the pigeons at Trafalgar Square
Visit the waxworks if you dare.

But when all is said and done,
And tourists in their thousands come.
Where can compare to what it's got
None - because London has the lot.

M Barker

HISTORY OF LONDON

London is a nice place with its wonderful green parks and space
where you see tourist with a smile on their face
or you could go to St. James' park to name but a few
what about Buckingham Palace or Kew
there's Westminster and Eros the statue
watch the plays at the theatre too.

Terry Croft

ODE TO THE DRIVER OF THE W3

The queue stretches out along the railings
Breath steaming way, way up, under the canopy
Dank cold air ribboned only by whiffs of warm and smelly diesel smoke
and slowly exhaled cigarettes
gripped tight in freezing fingers.
They come in ones and twos
now severally
to slump in line
waiting to be taken home
Some from work
Some from shows
and always those who seem to wander aimlessly about the Universe.
Minutes tick audibly by.
The driver, that Captain of our bus,
that driver, comfortful,
in his cab just feet away,
gets out his paper, holds it high, unfurled
across his line of vision -
pretends he doesn't notice us,
crouched, pale frozen ghosts
who might be passengers and fellow travellers
quite, quite soon -
oh God, let it be soon,
warmed and friendly once again.
And still he teases us.
How long should we support this dismal wait?

But what if we were all
to disappear?
Just like that, into the thin cold air?
when he looks up -
No audience left
No fares to collect
No ghosts or passengers to be seen.

All vanished? No, it can't be true!
Sorry mate, - we've all gone home on the W2!

Chris Shirley Smith

THE NEW NIGHT SHIFT MANAGER

Into the subterranean depot realm, he parades
past the water fountain, coffee machine
and anti-influenza propaganda nodding at the occasional
suspicious worker,
sorting and packaging boxes,
who he recognises as inferior quality.

He's prepared to prove himself under pressure,
having been sent in by central headquarters
to increase production and lower wages.

Heels clicking,
he checks the dockets in the office,
organising over-time schedules,
smelling of baby oil and talcum powder,
hands on hips,
gold jewellery everywhere,
grinning like a hyena.

He assigns duties on the roster,
fingers glinting with maximum output potential,
shoulders sticking out of his blue suit,
white shirt and yellow tie.

Beneath the heating and ventilation,
he admires the activity around him,
having been replenished by his wife's
excellent cooking, braised steak and mushrooms.

Simon Robson

LONDON

The many ancient buildings to adorn our capital city
Could tell so many stories of intrigue and love and pity.
When a prisoner went through Traitor's gate, so 'tis said,
That never again was he seen in charge of his head!

Dick Whittington and his faithful cat, was called to be Lord Mayor,
The bells of Bow rang overland and made the message clear.
Buckingham Palace home of the Monarch, a building known so well.
The Houses of Parliament and Big Ben, that is the name of the bell!

10 Downing Street and guards on parade
The Cenotaph where the poppies are laid.
The sights and sounds of London in sun or inclement weather,
Will give so many happy dreams that they will last for ever.

Duncan Lavie

I LOVE LONDON

As I lean on London Bridge,
My arms are holding fast, the ridge,
The flowing Thames goes slowly by,
St. Paul's stands out in the sky
Then I walk along The Strand
Trafalgar Square where Nelson stands
There I am arms out wide
All the pigeons at my side,
Down I go to Oxford Street,
Bright lights and shoppers to meet,
And *Eros* there his bow and arrow,
Flower lady with her barrow,
And as I gaze around you see
London is the place for me.

Thelma Hynes

50 YEARS REMEMBERED

Visions flash before my eyes of that triumphant
Victory Day,
Peace upon our Island, that treasured day in
May.
Our teenage years had flown away amongst the
scourge of war.
The fears for loved ones absent, soon would
be no more.

Old London Town woke up once more, bright
lights and laughter gay.
Pearly Kings down Lambeth Way performed
a Gala Day.
Church Bells rang out, Ships Sirens blared
from Putney on to Bow.
St Paul's stood proud triumphant as we prayed
there meek and low.

Our King and Queen and family shared both joys
and grief.
Those six years of warfare were years beyond
belief.
The wartime youth will not forget who made our
Victory Day.
The British Bulldog breed of grit, on that
treasured day in May.

V Deacon

ADVICE TO A FOREIGN TOURIST IN LONDON

You'll need courage, a camera, loose change and a map.
It's sure to turn cold so remember a mac.
There'll be plenty to do and too much to see
From the Tower of London to Westminster Abbey.

When you travel, take the tube, a cab or a bus.
You must first hail the taxi and don't make a fuss
When another jumps in and the cab drives away
That's life! C'est la vie! is what you must say.

For the Changing of the Guard you'll need a good view,
And remember the British do like to queue.
Then a trip on the Thames. Oh no! It's raining again!
Tell me, how does this compare with the Seine?

A visit to Harrods, don't take a rucksack!
Shop for momentos, ready-wrapped to take back.
You'll be jostled and hustled all down Oxford Street
By traders with souvenirs and all sorts to eat.

At night, if you've recovered and don't want to rest,
There's the theatre with *Cats* or *Starlight Express*.
But remember there are places that you shouldn't go
If you don't want to spoil the still rosy glow.
Under the arches or by deserted doors
Wrapped in paper they sleep on cold, dirty floors.
There's a dark side of London which will fill you with pity
If you dare to discover its cardboard city.

So I hope you like London, that you'll visit again
And next time you come, I'm sure it won't rain.
What do you think of this city with its sometimes grey skies,
You, who view London with a stranger's eyes?

Janice Fixter

CHILDHOOD MEMORIES

Rows of small grey houses
Looking tired and worn,
Inhabited by folk
Spirited and determined,
Picking up the threads of life
Making the best of things,
In the East End of London
Following the 1939-45 war.

Children lively and mischievous
Playing various street games,
Exploring forbidden bomb sites,
Spending pennies on comics, sweets,
No time to be lonely or bored,
Visiting the cinema, a treat,
Through the eyes of a child
A magical place.

Life, a struggle at times,
Dramas acted out, for all to see
Had its comical and fun side,
Parties held in traditional style,
Revellers spilling out into the street
Everyone jovial, content for a while,
Singing, dancing, well into the night
Wrapped in the warmth of the community.

Georgine Theobald

MANY A CONTRAST

A place of many a contrast,
The big and sometimes small.
Buildings of great beauty,
We'll visit one and all.

But slum conditions, also,
Prevail like mighty sea.
And must affect the picture
For both you and sometimes me.

We are proud of local monuments,
Where rich and famous dwell.
The Queen and Prince Philip
Are doing very well.

But think again of bag folk,
they wander to and fro,
Having no home, no friend and
Just no place where to go.

There's many a sad story
Of young folk, not a few.
Who find their way to London,
For a life that's bright and new.

Judith Mudd

SILVERTOWN

Ah, Silvertown, behind your smile I have found your silver.

There, embedded in the earth like a mirror glinting and gleaming
flows our nation's best known and beloved River Thames.
Steel cranes, standing erect, like silent sentries in salute
to a gracious past, whose banks once boomed and bustled with
cargo and ships, and in the pockets of seamen jingled real
sixpence's, florins and half-crowns too.

Now, nestled by its bank is found City Airport whose silver birds
rise like royal stevedores to destinations near and far.
And in the distance can be seen straddled from bank to bank
giant steel barriers put there by wise men to curb its power
should it become enraged.

In that factory over yonder, Tate & Lyle I mean, a female voice
rents the silence in syllables clear to inform; command; request.
Incessantly on flow minuscule sugary-grains that sweetens,
for you and me, our morning tea.

Whilst undisturbed flows that mighty river to its home, the Sea.

Mary Brown

A WINTER'S MORNING IN CHELSEA

Angels must have visited that night
whilst people were sleeping fast,
The sun bore down; sky clear blue,
A white miracle had been cast.

Sharp frost engulfed this London day,
Embankment sparkling lights,
Trees encrusted in the quiet cold,
Blue shadows   magical sight.

Then soft mist engulfed the wondrous scene,
now mysterious in shadowed haze,
They watched and marvelled with great joy
at nature's changing ways.

Old Thames beamed as the mist arose,
Sun shining through again,
River green rippling with deep delight
reflecting the wonder of men.

Jill Isaac

THE UNDERGROUND SONG

In the rush hour on the Underground in London town,
I let my trousers drop to the floor,
Caused delay, wasn't dangerous, didn't obstruct the door.

As I write from my hospital bed,
After the doctors had tampered with my head,
They say no more, will I drop my trousers to the floor
In public places,
            But I may pull faces.

Leslie Wakerell

HIGHGATE PAST

Cornfields and pastures and pleasant cool streams;
Extensive thick forest, so lush and so green.
Stags, boars and wild bulls and plenty of game;
Yes, Highgate today is not quite the same!
Then, thieves, robbers, outlaws and fugitives too,
Swamped the forest with danger for all who passed through.

Adjoining the forest a common is found.
In a deep dell a plague pit, a huge burial ground.
In the Great Plague of London, sixteen sixty-five,
Many corpses were brought here by those who survived.
Then up Highgate Hill, an old cemetery looms,
With old vaults, catacombs and gigantic great tombs.

In 1809 a large tunnel was cut
Over three hundred yards through the heart of the hill, but
Through influx of water on sand soil and gravel,
The whole thing fell in; 'twas the cause of the trouble.
In the wake of this fall Archway Road was then made;
The beginning of road-making was now firmly laid.

Up Highgate Hill is a caged stone that tells
Of Dick Whittington's call at the sound of Bow Bells.
What a view of old London we get from the top;
What a fantastic history. We can learn such a lot.
What great homes, inns of fame we have to relate
From the heart of this town, O, delightful Highgate!

P Burton

FRIENDSHIP

Friends are there to give a hand
When the going it gets tough
They put up with our foibles, and they
Forgive us should we huff.
To go through this world without a friend
To me paints a picture of hell.
It would make one feel like a tumbleweed
Or perhaps a n'er-do-well.
You only find out who your true friends are
When the chips are really down
They stand by to give encouragement,
The impostors are gone with a bound.
Friendship is like an invisible cloak that
Protects us from the cold.
It's a tonic that raises our spirits high
And it's worth much more than gold.

T McGinley

LOVERS MEET

If we meet some day on the street avoid my gaze.

Look away as though you didn't recognise me.

If my name is mentioned, act as if it never resounds in your memory.

For your soul and mind belongs to some one else other than me.

Parveen Dharr

THE ONLY ECHO

No dream makes any sense,
a dream is a foolish notion.
Dreamers will always dream alone,
no time can change what is now.

Wait an unplanned suffering,
a fruitless search with no goals.
Life goes on unheeded through time,
we will stand as tall as God allows.

Wait with me in the shadows,
I stand as naked as skin on bone.
Taken from my home, ripped away,
see my inner soul rages pain.

Darkness waits to conceal me,
your eyes see through the shadows.
I understand we all must find love,
we are as lonely as each other.

Blindness will consume my vision,
of you my eyes travel through time.
Hold a desperate man closely,
he only wants what he gives in return.

I am still. Motion is slowly subdued,
my heart beats as my mother inside.
Feed me with your bountiful words,
of you, I will eat only of the whole.

Richard Pinchen

THE LETTER

From London:

Affectionate thoughts I stir in his mind,
Of his lovely wife he had left behind.

With a pen and paper he brings me alive,
Expressing his love on my numerous lines.

He puts me in a post box as quick as he can,
And soon I join hundreds in a little red van.

I'm sorted and packed, then put on a plane;
Once more I continue my journey again.

Mile after mile we cover in haste;
I can't wait to see the joy in her face.

The postman walks ever so slow,
I earnestly wish the man would go!

At last he slips me through her door,
Then she picks me off the floor.

Her happiness flows as she reads me through;
How excited I feel when I bring good news.

: With Love

Gilbert Sofeso

SEASONS

I hate this time of year it's all in-between
not summer not winter if you know what I mean
you wake every morning dark and wet
then all depressed and miserable I get
Washing in machine I can't put it out
Can't get it dry, no dry clothes the family shout
I like winter with snow on the ground
Walking through it making a crunching sound
I like spring with flowers in bloom
the time of the year when you clean the room
but summer I like it the best
it's so much better than all the rest
it makes me feel happy with sun shining bright
Still bright as day 9 o'clock at night
So hurry up seasons get yourselves done
Let's get to May give me some sun!

Linda Holmes

THE LONDON BUS

The London bus - double deckered and red
May need to be a different colour instead.
Become single deckered and called *city bus*,
All these threats are creating a terrible fuss.

Ministers rage in Parliament Square
On losing a part of our heritage there.
Stating, 'London will risk losing part of its fame
For without its red bus it will not be the same'.

For Londoners too, this may cause angry tears.
Red buses have been with us now, ninety years.
A familiar sight which welcomes you -
The red London bus as it comes into view

Joan Manwaring

A BLINKERED VIEW OF LONDON

London, dear London.
A place full of dreams.
Buckingham Palace
the home of the Queen.
Piccadilly Circus
has bright lights that beam.
At Trafalgar Square
Christmas tree lights gleam.
Leicester Square
with films on big screens.
Tennis at Wimbledon
with strawberries and cream.
Concerts at Wembley
full of screaming teens.
So much to do,
So much to be seen.
London, dear London.
A place full of dreams.

Or is it?

E Flynn

DEPARTURE - GOING AWAY

I'll be missing you but
If I had to look you in the eyes
And say my love
I have to go
Please believe in me
I'll stay true to you,
Although
I will be miles away
My love will still stay true
Keep your love for me
On my return, which I will give to you
As it is a space of time in passing
It soon will pass my darling
Then we can wander by
Again in fields of love
And chase the past
To catch the love
You thought that you had lost
So my darling do not cry
Do not sigh
For I will soon be home
To stay with you
And in your arms once more
And never more will roam.

T E Lake

LONDON'S GOLD

They say that London's pavements
Are really lined with gold.
And you could make your fortune
Well, that's what I was told.
So off I went, to take a look
And much to my dismay
All the streets were just like ours,
Just slabs all dark and grey.
But then at night to my surprise
The city glowed, before my eyes.
The pretty lights had been turned on,
And all the streets, well they just shone.
the shops and theatres were so bright,
It really was a marvellous sight
Now I believe what I was told
The sights were worth much more than gold.

P Catchpole

HAMPSTEAD FAIR

The fairground across the hill
Blazed merrily with spinning wheels
Adorned with shining coloured lights
And children yelled tonight! tonight!

By morning all was gone
The fair had moved on
On the ground were bits of sparkling glass
A shattered illusion if ever there was one.

David Moir

ROOFTOPS

Muffled barking
of alloyed wheels snapping at rails,
a generous window seat
on a Richmond train
and London is a jigsaw of rooftops;
arranged in rows, they ride
independently across the skyline
of West Hill.

Here, a Victorian attic protrudes
above Edwardian chimney pots
and compulsory praying mantis TV aerials .

Miserably, they mutter
and curse the temperate climate
on a shivering mid-winter Sunday,
grey as the slates that cover them,
that yesterday shone,
mirrors - after recent rainfall.

Robert Ford

CITY SPIRES

Where, long ago, elegant spires in number raised their many and
                                                      varied heads.
Where each and every building had an individual shape.
Where man once pursued his many crafts.
Where the River Thames was a great vein, a true Father, not just
                                 a name, serving man and his trade.
Where markets were several and meat travelled on its hoof.
Where horse and a cart and sweat of a brow got you about.
Where man held his God in awe and there was not a car or motor-
                                                 cycle in sight.
Not so very long ago.
What of this city remains?
Why, a fort and a monument to a great blaze?
A few old spires, they remain, cramped in an overcrowded modern bed.
What remains?
Ghosts from under its counterpane.

P Young

LONDON BUTTERFLIES

Wings of yellow dance away,
At the dawning of the day
Glistening yet, still with the dew
Flying on to flowers new.
There beside a railway siding,
Shafts of glory are abiding
Which waken to the sun
From which fresh colours come.
Wings of mauve and wings of red,
Awaken from their sleepy bed
Blessing now the sunny hours
To frolic in amongst the flowers
And like small blossoms they can fly
Falling, drifting from a London sky.

Jenny Linehan

THE CITY OF LONDON

London is a lively city.
All the shops looking very pretty.
Big historical buildings looking all so regal.
Buildings like St. Paul's Cathedral.
The Houses of Parliament overlooking the River Thames,
Just along the way stands Big Ben.
Walking along the Embankment lit up at night,
Looks a glorious sight.
Little cafes on every street corner.
Lots of people come to London City,
Lots of sights, looking very pretty.
Then we have Madam Tussauds just up the road,
Then there's Pudding Lane, another story to be told.
Another place is Trafalgar Square,
People feeding the pigeons, they don't care they just fly everywhere.
Traffic going around Hyde Park,
Soon it will be very dark.
Sparkling lights to light the way,
Soon it will be another day.
Oh, what bliss
That London should look like this.
Up the road is Buckingham Palace, as it stands in all its glory.
I hope you enjoyed my story,
Of the City called London.

C Payne

THE SLEEPER ON THE BENCH

In the public gardens
among the lunching workers, he lay
Prone:
along a bench
Asleep!

They sat well away
as if
Fearing contamination by proximity.
Yet he looked not a tramp
Despite the bottle adjacent on the floor!

Clothed from head to toe in palest blue
Short hair, clean face,
trimmed beard.
He was a paradox unanswered:
but condemned by sleep!

C M O'Connell

GET TO KNOW YOUR HARINGEY

John Major may be a Brixton boy,
But I am truly Tottenham bred,
He may say back to basics,
But I've got other things in my head,
He calls it a classless society;
Yet there's a big difference still,
Between the deprivation of West Green Road,
And the smiles of Muswell Hill.

Joanne Chadwick

LONDON'S ALIVE

To take a cruise on the River Thames,
embark at Waterloo Bridge,
the sights passing by
leave all with a smile
history unfolds in your midst.

To take of a beverage at an old London pub
you'll see they're easy to find
traditional ale
a pint or a pale
go easy, you'll need your mind.

To take a walk in Covent Garden,
entertainment and things to buy,
sit down, have a drink
take a rest from your stint
and watch all the sparrows fly by.

To take in a show at the West End,
Mousetrap or Starlight Express,
there's fun for all
the circle or stall
It's always show-time up West.

But now alas, my ode must end
for I have no further to hide,
don't take it from me
just go and see
you'll agree that London's alive.

P W Jones

LONDON LIFE

There's a famous market
Where the traders all go,
Down to Petticoat Lane,
They sell their wares from tables and chairs,
Canopies to hold off the rain,
Cockney people will give you a smile
Tourist how nice to meet you,
A pub down the Lane,
Your visit again
Down the Old Cobbled Street they will greet you
There's buses and trains,
Day trips to, souvenir shops, see a show
Take a photograph or too,
It's all there for you.
London is the place to go.
After the day, you will always say
In London there's so much to do.
At night what a beautiful sight.
London lit up, what a view.

S Stuart

METROPOLIS

London flings the gauntlet down
At the upstart challenge of any town
Attempting to claim equality;
Despising all mediocrity.
Assured in its own renown.

Where else in the world such a tapestry
Rich woven with threads of history?
Its grimmer secrets darkly cloaked
In the ancient tower steeply soaked
In everlasting mystery.

Its fairer face, with sprawling smile
Entraps the visitor with its guile.
Turn here, turn there, turn anywhere;
Some magic force is in the air,
Defying definition's trial.

What diversity the traveller greets
Of varied structure. What competes
With London parts that sprawl serene,
A havened calm of green, between
The myriad of mingling streets.

All human endeavour here is found.
The arts; the sciences abound
As evidence of man's advance
Through life's long gallery of chance
To spheres of knowledge firm and sound.

History, majesty, age and modernity
Blended together in one vast reality,
London - the conquering hero of old
Whose streets are still running with buckets of gold
Reaches its arms to eternity.

Brenda Soderberg

MOVING TO KENSINGTON

From Enfield Town to a Kensington square,
At one time I thought I'd never get there.
What with being gazumped and buyers dropping out,
But that I would move I had no doubt.
At long last it came, the removal day,
A nightmare of course as they always say.
The removal men seemed to be not too sure
Of where to go and what is more
When they arrived at my new flat
Said, 'Flat nine? The top? We suspected that!'
All day they struggled up the stairs
With beds and tables, china and chairs,
And finally the cooker came,
Oh dear, I felt sorry, it was a shame.
It was June and such a steamy day.
I gave them a tip and could only say,
'Perhaps later you could have a beer,
Thank you so much for getting me here,
I've waited so long to achieve this goal.'
They smiled but said to each other, 'Poor soul,
We've had to climb up all day, OK
But she's got to live here everyday!'
They were right but I tell you I have no regrets,
The longer I'm here the easier it gets.
And I'm fit as a fiddle and slim as can be.
Who said London living was not so healthy?

Pauline Mills

KENSINGTON GARDENS

Through the entrance of the Palace Gates
people come in for their lunch time breaks,
Off with the bowlers, roll up the sleeves
time to enjoy a sandwich of cheese.

Such a lovely day, the sun shines bright
a gentle breeze, the children fly kites,
They bob and dance, tails flap in the wind
'Hold on tight', don't let go of the string.

There are *doggies* too, all shapes and sizes
who chase after squirrels and make barking noises,
Red-coated pensioners sit on the benches
chuckling at memories of boyhood adventures.

Joggers and cyclists exercise here
puffing and panting in their colourful gear,
Builders who've slogged with buckets and bricks
laugh and joke with a football for kicks.

By the Serpentine Lake, ducks and geese paddle,
at the first sign of bread, up to you they will waddle
Delighting the nanny with Edward and Claire,
Peter Pan in his garden with rabbits and hare.

With its fountains and bandstand and broad rhododendrons
How we love this oasis called Kensington Gardens.

Lucy Ambrose

THE SLEEPING MAN

The sleeping man is but a
travelling man
within the archives of his mind
are all the choices
that will lead him to
familiar things
or to the unknown longed
for destination of dreams
so
Silently - silently he sleeps
remembering with hope and affection
friends who brought him their gifts
of
their poetry of emotions
sometimes there were those who with
their hidden movement within
offered him a little of everything
this then is his piéce-de-resistance
conjuring up their very existence
dream, dreaming of all these then
and with each and every journey he makes
inspires him, as an artist within,
for warm comfortable places aren't everything.
The sleeping man is but a travelling man
sit down, slow down, and rest
nothing must be missed
he's part of all this,
the sleeping, travelling man.

Sharon Halsey

HELEN AT THE BUS STOP

She was the light of my life, the apple of my eye,
Waiting at the bus stop for the number sixty five.
I, the gallant knight, cruising in my steed of steel,
Decided to relieve her of this arduous ordeal.

I glided smooth and fast, straight in there like a dream,
Swerving quickly up the kerb, into an upright beam.
The bus stop was unmoved, people ran in all directions,
Helen stood there somewhat fazed by my interjection.

I pushed my car off the stop, collecting various bits and bobs,
I offered her a lift, making the best of a rotten job.
She graciously declined, suppressing giggles of girlish laughter,
This was not a tale of *Guy meets Girl, lives happily ever after.*

Kevin King

HAMMERSMITH REACH

The Thames seems to flow into all our poems -
that reach of river from boatman's memorial past
the playing fields of St. Paul's where the path
fritters away in a verge of wilderness.
The far side house-trained with tall chimneys
and warring red and yellow roses,
the pub stops that we know so well:
Blue Dragon, Rutland, Dove, Ship, Black Lion.

Flux, flux, soft as a brand of soap
the river breathes heavy in the heat.
We order ploughman's on the flags
and ox-eyed lager melting froth.
Scull and oarsmen block the towpath
like lollipop men in rowing strips.
The tideway ruches in its curtains.
Time for one more pint, one more poem.

Michael Henry

LIVING IN LONDON

Look out of your window,
Into the street,
There are so many people you'll never meet.

Hustle and bustle,
Lots of big crowds,
Pigeon droppings on the tops of tall towers.

Plenty of traffic,
Lots of fumes,
If you have asthma your life will be gloom.

Living in London's
Not as bad as it seems,
The busy capital is full of green trees.

Late night shopping
In Harrods or Boots,
But not if you're homeless or have no roots.

Claire Edwards

OUR LONDON

London's the place to be
You can take a tip from me.
There's a lot that you can gain
If you go to Petticoat Lane.
And watch your interest grow
As you're strolling through old Bow.
There's so much more to see
You'll love London just like me.

Colin Allsop

ACTION REPLAY

Noisy cars with brakes and hooters
Souls ruled by vast computers
Lots of races - crowded places.
Troubled lives
No warm embraces
Children crying - nature dying
Pollution stifling.
Stop!
Silent cars with brakes - no hooters
No souls ruled - non- polluters.
Lots of races - crowded places.
Controlled lives.
With warm embraces.
Children laughing - nature thriving.
Pollution dying.

Hari J Elliott

LONDON

Small seasonal pleasures,
Cherry blossom in spring.

Changing light,
Boat on the Serpentine.

Small surprises,
Known face in a crowd.

Play of weather,
Streets in rain shine.

Tidal flow,
River and birds at slack water.

Changes of delight countering
the alienation of the city.

C R Malcomson

I WONDER WHO LIVES IN A HOUSE LIKE THIS

All the people in this town,
Walk with noses in the air,
Drive around in fancy cars,
House prices they compare.
The children go to private schools.
Horse riding in the gala.
Their dogs don't know how to walk,
As they are carried to the parlour.
Women go to hair consultants
Just to mingle with those in the know.
Receiving invitations,
To dinner parties they must go.
Interior designers, gardeners and au-pairs,
Just to let the neighbours know
Who's walking up one's stairs.
I keep telling my husband
It's hip to be called darling or bunny
He replies 'I'd better get off to work
To keep you in all this money.'

Traci Adams

LONDON - HELD TO RANSOM

London Transport - thy name should be shame,
Lateness and cancellations are thy claim to fame.

London Transport makes me late for work,
My boss watches the clock like a hawk.
If I am late once more,
I could be out of the door!

London Transport, you've kept my friends waiting and waiting,
I'm sitting in a tunnel when I should be celebrating.
I've missed dinner dates, concerts and plays.
London Transport's excuses - let me count the ways.

'There will be severe delays due to staff shortages.
Various underground stations closed due to water seepages.
New trains stuck in tunnels, incompatible with old track.'
Excuses, excuses, excuses are something L/T doesn't lack!

Living in London could really be a pleasure,
With so many ways to fill my leisure.
So come on London Transport get on the right track
And, please give me my rightful leisure time back.

J Carlsen

OUR GREAT LONDON

No wonder it is the capital to *behold*
What excitement and wonder to be told
The Trocadera and now TGI's
The limits and choice reaches beyond the skies
Madam Tussauds, Hard Rock Cafe and Oxford Street
Makes you feel weak being so on your feet.

Up the escalators and down the stairs
You'll see the cockney's calling them *apple and pears*
All the people what a buzz
Stand in the midst and feel the dust
Oh! When you've been you feel so elated
Worn out and tired but thoroughly *baited*.

You can't wait for the next visit of *going to town*
It feels like a drug, it calls you, when you are down
It does not matter if you're a girl or a bloke
When the weather gets bad, you can take off to the *smoke*
I would not live anywhere more remote
For if I was asked. I would think it a joke!

Jill O'Donnell

ARMISTICE DAY

The Garden of Remembrance off London's busy square,
Is packed with quizzy tourists who've only come to stare.
Oblivious of the people who jostle past her there,
A small, and bent old lady's the only one to care.

A cross, so small and simple, she carries in her hand,
In memory of her only son, who died far from this land.
Past rows and rows of crosses, she slowly makes her way,
And at each cross she pauses, on that bleak and windy day.

With footsteps far from steady, and eyes from age grown dim,
She peers at all the crosses to find the name of him.
In spite of all the people, who pass close by her there,
There is no one to help her, there is no one to care.

And so she struggles onward, oblivious of the crowd,
Her mind intent on finding, that name of which she's proud.
The cross at last she reaches whereon his name is borne,
And then she slowly places her cross into the lawn.

No one even notices the woman standing by
For just a moment's homage, a teardrop in her eye.
No friendly word of comfort, no kind or gentle smile
Was given to that woman, so lonely all the while.

Then on her way she wended, soon lost within the throng.
And no one would remember, or care where she had gone.

Rosy Jones

A VIEW

We drive in from the country
to a place called London Town.
It's always full of people
running all around.
We wonder where they're going and if
they ever stop,
To look at this great city they all
seem to have forgot.
There's history all around them
but they don't realise
because this modern life they
lead time just passes by.
Maybe they should stop a while
and have a look about
This lovely place called London
so much history all about.

Christine Licence

HAMPSTEAD HEATH

There's nothing more to give you a glow
than Hampstead Heath covered in snow.
Toboggan with adult trying to cope
as toboggan and child slide on down the slope,
The tall still trees with branches so white
glisten in sunshine and glow in moonlight.
Footprints decorate the once plain pathway
now hidden from sight by many who stray.
The playground quiet 'cept one creaking swing
the pool now so vacant awaiting the spring.
Vast grasslands so clean and bright to the eye
so peaceful, serene of a summer gone by.
Oh! For the heath, without you I fear
No more winter madness, no more summer cheer.

Carol Wilkins

A DAY IN THE CAPITAL'S FAIRGROUND

What kind of a place is this, as he stumbled off the train around a
                                                      quarter to eight,
and given a tube map showing routes from place to place.
Covent Garden, Charring Cross, Oxford Circus and Kings Cross.
And after a guided tour of each individual place,
with their own definition and own traditional markings of condition.
Like a fairground the choice is yours
as you approach a new founding
and step out of the darkness of the underground to new surroundings,
that lures the different species to their own unique set place.
But stop in the hustle and the bustle,
take a step back from this hungry pace
for some who find it a challenge can also lose their sense of balance
will spin into ten different ways.
Like a merry go round,
head whizzing round for London's pulse manifests
at a fast rate always taking the leading role for she if the capital
                                                      of all states.
London, London, London, *London* boy what a place.

Donna Pitt

A VISIT TO LONDON

No wonder people visit London from all over the world,
It's not for the sun because it's more often cloud,
But our capital is famous for so many things,
Like Big Ben's chimes echoing out very loud.

Bright lights and lots of people
Taxis, buses, trains and cars,
Shops, museums, houses,
Hotels, night-clubs, theatres and bars.

St. Paul's Cathedral, Covent Garden,
Markets - Bishopsgate, Smithfield, Petticoat Lane,
Downing Street, The Houses of Parliament,
People visit London again and again.

Chelsea Flower Show and Kew Gardens,
A stroll in Regents Park,
Or take a boat trip along The Thames,
See the lights at Christmas after dark.

Excited children up on daddies shoulders,
Horses, soldiers, perhaps a wave from The Queen,
It's The Trouping of The Colour,
It really must be seen.

Head buzzing, legs aching, feeling weary and tired,
London - Oh what a lot to see,
Why not finish the day off completely,
Perhaps The Ritz for a nice cup of tea!

B Archer

SUNSET ON WIMBLEDON COMMON

Jetliners score the golden sky.
A hundred memories rush by.
The windmill holds its silent sway,
As we sit here this summer's day.
Long shadows from the poplar trees
Extend their coolness to our tryst.
We lie on damp flat grass and touch
As though we had not touched that much.
Mosquitoes hum as Bowie sings,
Knowing not his words, just our skins.
A long time passes, and it is night.
A man is calling in the failing light.
'Jodie?' His dog perhaps.
It seems we've kissed for hours.
Our lips are sore and we are cold.
'Will it be like this, when we are old?'

Andrew Weston-Webb

A WINTRY LONDON

Traffic! Traffic! everywhere,
Life is just one great big dare,
Everything's in a hustle and a bustle,
Can't hardly stretch or move a muscle.

In the morning when you wake
the sun up there is just a fake
Cause it never starts to shine
till way past the hour of nine.

Sheila Nicholls

THE SHUTTLE

I've been travelling on a coach train
Looking out the window
Onto a misty meadow landscape
Responding to a signal that's calling me back
My mind working like a shuttle on a loom
Beating back glimpses of the past
To knit a knowledge of myself
Gathering skeins into bundles of belief -
Hopeful, doubtful, then again hopeful conviction
Of how to approach time's passage -
Separating threads of tangled memories
The mental shuttle relates lost faces, lost places
To forgotten elations, forgotten desperations
Trying to weave a tapestry full of significance for the present, the shuttle
Suddenly reels to a halt
Interrupted by the announcement of the next stop

Passengers burdened with cases of reminders
Sigh . . . then rush onwards
Their individuality lost in the throng of travellers
However on close examination
Captured in modes of meditation
Each face mirrors a different mood as
Each mind sorts the passing scenery
According to its own mysterious code

Monica Gurney

BIG CITY

It's night,
But everything is bathed
In neon orange.

I'm cold . . . alone.
Dropped like a piece of rubbish
In the street.

Does anyone know who I am?

No.

This big, big city
Swallows us up -
Trying to keep us out of sight.
We are embarrassing to people,
Who look the other way as they pass.

They live in a big city
But try to ignore the Big Issue.

Rebecca Smith

RUGGED IDENTITIES

In history
coal bucket
steel everything.

Now mainly motor noise
scrap
still rugged -
still Rotherham!

Colin Nixon

LONDON

London, Oh! London I hear you say
it's a tired old place that's dirty and grey
with hurrying people all numb with the race
of reaching the top and setting the pace
dressing up late to go on the town.
Their tired wan faces all furrow and frown

The city I know in a quite different light
I know it by day and I know it by night
The quaint little corners all quiet and shy
that tell us a story of ages gone by

The spirit of London lives on the Thames
which ripples and tumbles like sparkling gems
Acres of park land a wonderful sight
in Spring when the daffodils fill them with light

I know the people that live in this town
black and white and all shades of brown
They live in the suburbs in fashionable semi's
the live in the centre in flats for the many
High rise and low rise they never complain
although the lift's out of order again

When we're in trouble, my neighbours and me
whether it's sickness or sadness - you see
I know the people who come to our aid
with help and assistance and never get paid
They never give up and they never give in
in spite of the turmoil they sometimes live in.

The Cotswolds, Lake District and far Scottish Glens
are wonderful places to spend the weekends
but to live everyday with its ups and its downs
I'll opt for always for old London town.

H Penry

THE PAVEMENT ARTIST

I watch the workman place the paving stone
And, with a craftsman's dextrous care, smooth fine
The ridges of cement which blur the line
Between the butting slabs. These hands have grown
To callused prime in mastering their known
Accomplishment. Perhaps they could design
And execute mosaic, yet resign
Themselves impassively to what alone
Is needed for a busy London street:
A pavement artist to maintain the way
And cater for the heedless passing feet.
The chic shop windows offer their array
Of stylish artistry; yet none compete
With what the simple paving stones display.

Mary Spain

FROSTY MIDNIGHT. DULWICH WOODS

Who comes along the path at midnight,
Who, shrouded in cloak's fold?
While the wind moans and the moon glistens,
Who comes?

Two for comfort when the wind lashes.
Two for succour on the bleak way.
While the leaves sound to the frost's hammer;
Two come.

Crystal the tones the wind and the frost whisper.
Muffled the words that travel from cloak to cloak.
Brittled by rime, bruised are the bladed grasses:
They pass.

Mary Stella Ling

THE THAMES - OUR THAMES

The Thames, in southern England, is a river all should see!
Green lawns fringe its water;
weeping willows, flower pillows
and beds of blooms that caught the
sun and trapped it, all lie in tranquillity.

Boats a-bobbing at their moorings, swans dotted here and there;
lads longing for a catch of small fish.
Sagging lines seem, out in mid-stream,
loath to grant this very small wish
and yield only disappointing weed for those, so patient, waiting there.

Even when the fickle tide's out, there's a fascination still
in the mud along the foreshore.
Gnats and midges, jetties, bridges,
picnics, food and drink for more
little kiddies, looking wide-eyed, enjoying life as children will.

Yes! You'll find some dereliction, factory sites and office blocks,
wayward townies casting litter,
bits of flotsam - even jetsam -
cast-off clothing, cans of bitter,
but can you scorn the skill of sculling or mar the novelty of locks?

River Thames flow on forever! May your progress never end!
Demonstrate your peace and power,
change-resistance, pure persistence
day-by-day and hour-by-hour.
You possess the truest beauty as, majestically, your way you wend.

Fredrick West

LONDON

During final approach the wing dipped
and we looked down on Isleworth and Hounslow.
If it wasn't for the glint
of the Grand Union as we tilted,
it could have been a page from the A-Z,
that pilot of grid and labyrinth

that hides

the layers, the pump and movement beneath,
innards murmuring within a one-off brick hive
of flowing pipe and tunnel below the slabs
supporting the hum and mingle of island-civic
speckled with red bus, box, and tunic,
ripened by history, capitalised by Latin chisel,
belled by ermine and purple, whigite tempered,
guarded by unashamed, crapped on heroes
daring an invasion, ready to hoof off
dense plinths and down thoroughfares of stucco
rooted in the prints of stockinged burghers' feet
wet with loading hulls slopping on the river
pregnant with surge and staying-power

'We'll build here,' someone once said.

Adam Campbell

ODE TO WALTHAMSTOW

Just one century ago
This town we know as Walthamstow
Was just a lovely country village
Free from crime and greed and pillage
Where everywhere the gracious trees
Bowed pleasantly with every breeze
Where peace and quiet reigned supreme
A haven of delight, a dream
But now, all that has changed, I fear
Although we have a source of cheer
A thriving market in the street
At prices you will never beat
Attracting people from afar
The door to bargains is ajar
The forest's a mere mile away
Where one can spend a happy day
The river Lee meanders through
There is fishing, boating, swimming too
Our reservoirs can take small yachts
Canada geese arrive in flocks
With cormorants and herons too
Such lovely birds within our view
And on our marshes rare plants grow
It's lovely still, our Walthamstow!

Lillian Smart

THE TREE

Sheltered under the big tree
its strong trunk behind my back
its huge branch a canopy over my head
stark and black against the pale winter sky

Your strength contradicted
by a host of dainty leaves
dancing and murmuring in the wind.

You could be home
but for the nosy passers-by
you could be company
if we removed together into solitude
but here on a city Common
we are separated
by the furtive glances of the dog-walkers
which - unseeing and mindless - intrude

Thank you for your immovable strength
thank you for your whisper and dance.

Wanda Hayman

A CLEANER'S FAREWELL TO LONDON

I'll not return to ring monotony,
These railings polished finally shine.
These coffee stains they will not breed,
As other hands will do this deed.

I'll stand no more in pre dawn dark,
On Totil, Tower, Bank or Bow.
Begrudging guards who open doors.
Won't number me among their chores.

I'll run no more from stop to stop,
First buses too infrequent few.
Or lose my eyes through glassy pane,
To sweet relentless London rain.

I'll never live this age again,
On London's streets a painful youth.

Jerome David

UNTITLED

Over London I look, into the distance I stare,
From Buckingham Palace to Leicester Square.
On this column I have stood from 1842,
Surveying London's ever-changing view.
From horses to cars and buildings so tall,
Many the changes - I've seen them all.
This city I love so well and so dear,
This city that endures from year to year.
Four lions guard me no fear have I,
As I spy London with my left eye.

Andrew Ebrahim

A DOG'S TALE

I cannot understand the logic of the human race,
They talk about *a dog's life* as if it's some disgrace.
Dumb animals, they call us, how insulting and unkind,
We're really quite intelligent, as all our owners find.
And when the postman calls, we say 'good morning' with a bark.
Misunderstanding, he walks off and with some snide remark.
So who's dumb now? Our friendly effort is not understood,
We only want to shake his paw, we'd tell him if we could.
But he just makes unfriendly noises, seems to be afraid
And doesn't quite appreciate the gesture we have made.
But as an individual, I'm happy with my lot
And I'm extremely grateful for the comfort I have got.
A spacious house with room to move, I live a lovely life
Am very well looked after by my master and his wife.
We live near Epping Forest, go exploring every day,
Enjoy the freedom, without leash, where I can romp and play.
It's so exciting roaming round with lots of lovely trees,
Which is an added bonus as each well trained dog agrees.
And as for fouling paths, I think the owners are to blame,
For they should teach a code to pets, consider their good name.
If humans want to own a dog, I really think it best
That *they* should have a training session, pass a canine test.
I'm lucky, for I have a master who's beyond reproach,
A caring man, who's kind and gentle, has the right approach.
He knows I am his friend and I would never let him down,
Behave as he would wish me to, in country or in town.
Besides, I have respect for him and other people, too,
And wag my tail with pleasure when they approve of what I do
But some dogs just don't know the rightful way to go about,
But I've a master who is proud of me when I go out!

Norah Carter

A SPRING WALK BY THE TOWER OF LONDON

Throned in the midst of grimy city streets.
Only a moment's walk to restful calm,
To where small groups of children off from school
Or camera clicking tourists come to view.
From Tower Hill where speakers daily plead
A brief release from insignificance.
Now down across the street towards the tower.
Outside, where still the sentry's watch is kept
Just for tradition's sake. Onward we walk
Along the cobbled pathway, passing rows
Of ancient armaments, and little plots
Of crocus covered grass; and gaze with awe
At time worn battlements of what was once
A mighty fortress. Where now the pigeons
Enjoy their winged supremacy, and take
Advantage of their generous natured guests.
Then, just beyond the path, the silver sheen
Of sunlight dancing on the River Thames,
To cast illusion on its muddy flow,
Unruffled save by steamer's furrowed wake.
Then onward, underneath the bridge itself
Where land and water cross, with siren blast
The ship goes through. We now retrace our steps,
For we must leave and all is lost to view.

John Christopher Cole

ALL GIGS ARE OFF

One of those places where
Creased men and stained women
Sit round the walls and
Don't talk, just drink.

By nine, when we turned up,
They were well on, silent
And unpredictable.
I said I didn't like it,

Mostly men in the back bar,
Hard day workers,
They took their music like whiskey;
To stun their boredom

And there's always one,
This time a thin woman
In tight grey jeans, seamed
And smoked out,

Who howled at us
From the first beat,
Making everyone shift
And glance with nerves.

Hamish, who booked us in,
Got knifed last week.
Over here from South Island,
To see what the old country

Had to show
And earning a bit,
He's dead.
That was close.

All gigs are off.

Chris Hardy

WAITING AT THE BUS STOP

Waiting at the bus stop
For the same old bus
Others join me
People that are fat,
        or thin,
               or tall,
                      or short,
                            or demented.

Soon they leave
on the next bus

More people arrive
People wearing black
               or white
                      or green
                           or red
                               or kimonos

Soon they leave
on the next bus

leaving me
and my shadow.

Janine Holder

ALL RAILWAYS LEAD TO LONDON

From trading-post to commercial metropolis,
From Roman Londinium to Augusta,
In glory and in splendour, in ever-lasting lustre,
    All railways lead to London.

Once the heart of a vast empire,
Having lived through wars, two plagues and a fire,
Strewn with tree-lined avenues and cobble-stoned pavements,
    All railways lead to London.

A warm-hearted city that'll never grow cold,
An abyss of tales, yet to be told,
Of history, culture, yet to divulge,
    All railways lead to London.

As the setting sun's rays smile upon him,
The lingering righteous lover, in dismay,
In insatiate yearning, will stumble and stray,
    All railways lead to London.

And so, as the sinning delinquent
Strives to make this world a bitter one,
In radiant beauty, London shall battle on.
    All railways lead to London.

A city you'll never grow weary of,
    London.

Rafael Kimberley-Bowen

PROGRESS

Spring

For almost three hundred years it stood on Wanstead Green
It really was a sight to be seen
In Spring the buds were filling out
It looked so good you wanted to shout.

Summer

In Summer the chestnuts were plentiful
The squirrels ate until they had had their fill
People sheltered under the boughs from sun and rain
Alas, no more, it's such a shame.

and *Fall*

It stood in the way of the Link Road
And sadly no remorse was shown
When the bulldozers moved in and made it fall
What price progress? was the call!

Sheila Watkins

2010

From Victoria to Elizabeth the Second,
That iron fist of real monarchical power;
Has ruled the working class of dear old London Town
And therefore sir - the working class
Of dear old London Town
Has been ruled - therefore and because
By those yuppie Tory *chaps*.

There were Anarchists then,
And there's Anarchists now;
And soon - those rivers of blood?
But nay!
More than simply rivers of Blood
In the year of number 2010
For then the Tory harvest of '94 - will be reaped.

For as my forbears; those brave men
Of Tolpuddle - in Dorset;
Dared ask for meagre increase in their wage
Then now - the proud and utter dear working class
Of London town - that hold this England together.
As one - will indeed, rise up to state, 'We've had our fill,
Of this Tory rubbish and bilge' -

Victoria's children's children;
Are now the Tory *chaps*, -
Who ruined our London in sixteen years.
The dates, 'I'm sorry sir, - 1978 - '94.'
Well! Now the new inheritance - another sixteen years
This time - Elizabeth's divorced, children's children?

R Redmond

CARDBOARD CITY

Past the terraced houses, onwards to the city gates

we have some brand new buildings on entering The Strand and forward to Temple Gate.

Some are small, some are large

And some no roof at all.

There are lines of cardboard boxes all in zig zag lines

Which have only been seen in modern times.

The purchasers try to sleep with hope and tortured minds

Some wishing they had not been born and some sorry they are still alive

Rats brown and grey come up from sewers deep

Beneath the ground to inspect these cardboard boxes

Which are disturbing them with cardboard sounds and funny noises

Some as big as large tom cats

Walking tall and proud like city gents

Wearing fur coats, but alas no top hats.

When it's time to wake at dawn and with despair, the nightmare will go marching into day

The only consolation it's getting warmer for it's the glorious first of May.

Morning comes police arrive to move these squatters off
kicking hard to end of box

Heads shoot out like children's Jack in the Box

but not with smiling faces, just sad looks and voices

saying what do you want.

Charles E Watford

HOPE

If there's a time there's a world.
If there's a world there's a time.
Will peace and harmony ever combine?
When the river is deep, I will be strong.
The wind will guide me,
And I'll know where I belong.
Will you be there to help me through?
I know I'll be there to care for you;
Will you pick me up if I fall?
Will you break down the barrier,
Break down the wall?
For that wall is life;
And life is ours -
Destiny holds so many powers;
'Always and Forever' is what they say,
I won't give up,
I'll find my way . . .

Henrietta Hersh

RAVENSBURY

A profusion of sound.
Is it left, or is it right?
Water gurgling through its pipes - rapid, noisy gurgling.

The walls - virtually non-existent.
Row upon row upon row of house.
Row upon row of sound.

Voices in the background,
Humming through the walls.
Only not soothing, not vaguely hypnotic,
Irritating, scraping,
Like the heels of the voices carried on the pavement below.
Like the slamming of the car doors,
Or the engines going over the humps in the road.
Slowing down, speeding up, changing down, changing up.
All as close to blow away the papery glass
From the frames of the window,
And to bite into your ear
A frighteningly loud whisper,
So clear, so sharp
As to leave the moisture from its lips
On your lobes for the rest of the day,
Indeed for the rest of the year.

Samantha Mardell

MY STREET

So close to town, yet so far away, lined by trees, not a
motorway.

Tree branches entwine and often embrace, like lovers
meeting in a secret place.

Their colours change from green to red until their leaves
fall and are finally dead.

Bullocks still wander slowly down the road, into the gardens
causing havoc untold.

Munching their way through expensive blooms while the owners
watch helpless from their living rooms.

Mr Pierce takes his dog for a walk always willing to stop
and have a long talk.

Henry his dog sits patiently by waiting to catch his owner's
eye, longing to continue his little jog, after all he is a
boisterous dog.

It's a pleasant road wide and sleek, not at all run of the
mill like the next street.

Linda Farrell

LONDON

London is a busy place,
Movement all over the place,
The cars are beeping,
And people are rushing,
Bobbing in, bobbing out.
People in the street off to work,
Some in taxis,
Some on the tube,
But every one's rushing in their own kind of way.
Taxis are trying to earn their pay.
Buses booming down the street,
Stopping all over the place.
Oh London is a busy place.

Philip Meikle

TWILIGHT IN RICHMOND

Velvet tints of mauve streak overhead,
The golden globe begins his fall,
Before he finds his bed,
We watch the fading ball.

A muted song now fills the air
Of birds preparing for the night.
The parting of the clouds
Leaves sky quite bare,
With only branches left in sight.

I take your hand in quiet peace,
Our years are falling too.
But though the light will quietly cease
My twilight stays with you.

Hazel Turner

SOLD FOR BUILDING PLOTS

The wood has gone the land lies bare
with saddened eyes I stop and stare.
Once here were trees and hedges green
a little brook ran in between.

A foot path through the wood did lead
to brambles all entwined with weed.
To lovely ferns and willow bay herb
and black birds nests we'd not disturb.

We gathered elder flower for wine
and children played here most the time.
A rubbish dump with nettles tall
old mans beard hung over all.

Elms though dead stood tall and proud
their branches bare beneath the cloud.
Oak and Maple - Silver Birch too
would harmonise when strong winds blew.

In Autumn all the crispy leaves
would flutter from these lovely trees
and form a carpet on the ground
a joy to walk on for the sound.

But all is lost - gone for good
our trees and hedges - our wood.

Now when I come here - I look round and see
houses have sprung where our wood used to be.
Two large blocks of garages stand there on the ground
where Oak trees and hedges once did abound.

The houses are pretty looking all fresh and new
with flowers in gardens - where tall ferns once grew.
Children now live there - and together they play
echoing sounds from our wood - of yesterday.

Now Sedgewood Close

Jean M Eyre

THE LAST TRAIN

Here I sit deep in the tunnels of speed.
To disappear, or to reappear.
The chattering around me.
The unpunctuality surrounding me.

The noises, the silent rumbles;
The approach of the train of destiny,
Halts itself in my vision of the future.
Where will it take me?

I know not this until I reach the far off land.
A city run by a judicial system of eternity.
The boredom, the anger, the fear.
Hypothetical nerves sensed in my darkest thoughts -

Where am I?
Indeed I do not know.

Fantasies of life appear in my open mind;
Escapism it might be . . .
Escapism from where? I ask myself.

Matthew Hersh

STRATFORD EAST

Stratford - or should I say Stratford East,
the name has become a bit of a beast,
but my old town is really just the same
uninspired by its new town name.
Stratford has a centre - a gentle beating heart,
no throbbing masses - more a jam tart.
It has all the shops and a market, what's more,
and a one way system with the church as its core.
The people are real with always a word,
friendly and human, and often absurd.
So what has Stratford more than most?
What is its treasure that residents toast?
Its tree lined roads are pleasant it's true,
but the parking's a hazard, boxed-in, stuck like glue.
All the terraces differ - stone clad or bricked,
some all done up or with paint, barely licked.
Unkept hedges or gardens of flowers,
some derelict, others spent hours.
Stratford's not boring, nothing is uniform,
but the air turns foul when it gets warm,
So what makes it special, a diamond to me?
There appears to be nothing and no guarantees.
What makes it worth a mention in rhyme?
You must visit the place, come anytime,
and remember me, a resident here,
extolling the virtues of Stratford with care.
For someone to praise a town for itself
forgetting it's poor - for that is its wealth,
We've done the best within our means,
giving dignity to all Stratford's scenes.

Robert S F Young

FATE AND FATALITY

Here in the fire,
Now is the past,
As death survives first,
And life follows last.

With beauty in mountains,
The grey dawns of belief,
Arise noble torment,
And signal relief.

And behind powdered hearts,
Lies grief beckons hate,
But ever uncertain,
To be early or late.

For somewhere 'tis great,
Devils need not want,
To fall foul of flames,
Like the servants in front.

And so too passion,
Cold flickers of dusk,
The burning of evening,
Of ashes to trust.

Calling to die,
Scorch Lucifer's soul,
Into the fire,
Young into old.

Chris Hamlin

A WALK IN THE WOODS

It is peaceful in the autumn woods.
I am the only walker here away from the path.
I watch the quiet descent of leaves
Accumulating on the forest floor.
The curvaceous oak leaves and serrated sweet chestnut
Mingle haphazardly beneath my feet.
I enjoy the rustle as I kick the leaves
And re-live childhood memories.

Twigs snap beneath my feet
As dampness permeates my shoes
And numbs my toes through woollen socks.
Red-tinted brambles cascade in abundance.
The rough mottled bark of the silver birch shines.
Squirrels scamper from tree to tree
But freeze when they hear me approaching.
What tenacity of tenure
To hang sideways until danger passes.

In the distance, swans glide on a glittering lake,
Uptailed ducks forage for food,
Coots call quietly to their mates.
Moorhens swim silently, red beaks set determinedly.
The iridescent green of a drake's head fascinates me.
Suddenly a boy throws a stone, Splash!
Concentric circles form, enlarge and disappear
And the water fowl disperse.

Diana M Lock

OLD AND LONELY

What do we live this life for
So much hurt and pain
What do we live this life for
What do we hope to gain?

Old and lonely is what we become
After our life's love is gone
Living on our memories we slowly fade away
It hurts so much why should we stay?

Another day, another month, another year.
Still so lonely
I long to be with you dear.

Lesley Wright

THE BEGGER

So many people question me,
a lot are passers by.
They whisper to each other and they
stare and say 'Oh my.'
They see my rags and see my hair,
they look at me and frown, so
many of them are quite cruel they like to
put me down.
Sometimes I get a halfpenny, that's on a
lucky day.
Your luck is up you've got a coin,
that's what the rich folks say.

Catherine Whitehouse

ISLINGTON

My grimy heaven:
The Angel Islington
Where secret French cafes
Absorb lunch time tales
And red wine and candles
Are the order of the day.
The antiques arcade
Where one can browse
Over someone's old jewellery
And deals are made
Over chipped china cups
From decades ago . . .
Weaving and winding
In Chapel Street market
Try strawberries, raspberries
Herbal teas, joss sticks,
And exotic fish lie and
Fix you with their beady eyes
Or watch the world go by . . .
London office girls sit and dream
In Culpepper community park
Filled with fat velvet roses
And men wearing glasses.
Something for everyone:
The hectic streets
Where people flood
Or back-street oasis, yes
Islington
Is in my blood.

Karen Barnett

WALLINGTON

Its name at first was Waleton,
A place where strangers dwelt,
Prophetic words, for on this ground
An aerodrome was planned.

But counsellors in their wisdom
Eschewed the chance of fame.
Let the town of Croydon
Bear the airport's name.

Now where once the throb of planes
Started with the dawn,
Houses cluster round the field
Where history was born.

Each street recalls a hero
Or a well loved aeroplane
Early fliers, pioneers
Who made this place their own.

Mollison, Hinchliffe, Hermes
De Haviland and Roe.
Hercules and Kingsford
Names from long ago.

On the borough's coat of arms
Is a heraldic plane
Showing that Wallington still bears
A special claim to fame.

E Dimmock

ANOTHER SPRING

I've come to visit you today
To tell you things I know you'd say
If only you were here my dear,
To see with me that spring is here.
The wondrous beauty that abounds
Around us, all the sights and sounds.
Upon the ground wherein you lie,
Reaching upwards to the sky
A mass of colour has appeared,
To take the place of blossoms seared
By winter's harsh unfriendly blight,
As if by magic overnight.
Crocuses of every hue
Vie with hyacinths of blue
To catch the eye to hold to gaze,
Reminding me of halcyon days
We spent together you and I,
When we were young, and hopes ran high.
The rhododendrons by the brook
Beckon me to come and look
At buds, that strive with all their might
To burst into colour and add to the sight
Of life renewing, of joys still in store,
The wonder of spring is here once more.
And as I tell you of these things,
From quite close by a robin sings.
Perhaps to hear that song more clear,
A small grey squirrel ventures near.
He shows no fear, a friendly soul
And life's again not half, but whole.

M J Peachey

OUR MARKET

Right gals,
Here's a little puzzle for you;
Where can you save?
And hear Chas and Dave?
And meet the best people too?

Well it's Walthamstow High Street
Of course.
We can sell you some spuds,
We never sell duds,
We even could flog you a horse.

We're out here in the summer,
Autumn, winter and spring,
We stock toys for young tots
And all sorts of pots,
Although they might not all be Ming.

Now have you been to the pie shop?
Try the pie, mash and liquor too;
Or taste a fresh eel
If that doesn't appeal
And Sid's caff does a very nice brew.

Now this year we had Christmas lights.
Everyone said 'How nice'
'Please have them next year
When we come for our gear
And bargains at just the right price.'

Diane Hallsworth

EARLY MORNING DIPPERS

Shadows in the dark, cool smooth water,
An oasis, a sanctuary, a cold bath.
We meet before dawn
People I know in fractions, a piece of their lives
We have our reasons, all seasons,
Early morning dippers

First in, spreads a slow ripple, sometimes a sharp gasp
The water still, lies waiting to catch my breath.
It massages, soothes and eases my soul.
Occasionally it bites, deep into my skin.

Men with coloured hats swim step to step
Victorian ladies swim with grace, brushing islands of leaves
into circles.
We others patrol in lengths, trawling whirls and fine nets of
unsettled silt.

The clear blue softens and becomes still once more,
There are mats and flasks and steaming water bottles after, to
temper the icy hand that grabs your back taut and snatches
warmth away.

There are knowing smiles and simple exchange
With these people I have come to know, in part.
No real questions why.
At the hour of dawn, in the shadows of two worlds
We seem timeless and ageless.
The early morning dippers.

D J V Wright

GREAT GIANTS

As I walk through this park, in tow of my dog, a sight before me lies,
Great Giants of old slumber deep, beneath a weeping sky,
Some force unknown to man did come, so angry and so strong,
Causing death and distruction through the path it swept along.
It was an act of God they say, an act of the Devil more like,
Nowhere was sacred, nowhere was safe, no valley, hill, dale or dyke.

The Giants of old lay wearily, on sodden earth they wait,
For death to release them of their silent pain, caused by the winds of hate,
Giants still standing look down on their brothers,
In mourning they sway in the breeze,
A breeze now soft and caressing, dancing about branches and leaves.

My dog, unaware of the sadness, jumps over the tree trunks and logs,
Great limbs of the striken giants, who now lie in the laps of the Gods,
The seeds of the fallen heros litter the surrounding earth,
Waiting for mother nature to once again give birth,
To children of the Giants, that once stood proud and tall,
and brought so much pleasure and wonder to us all.

Stephanie C Rondeau

WHILE CONTEMPLATING LONDON

Beloved river, coursing through pulsating city,
Ever undulating to each nuance of lunar orchestration;
From some secret source you rise -
Though humble rural brook, you slowly swell; with careless grace
You ribbon through parochial countryside in quiet haste.
With fortitude you bear our thoughtless urban waste.
And lightly toss your sometime flotsam with generous panache.
With pageantry and style, our city grew around you,
Embracing you and dressing you with bridges.
Revered and respected your urgent weighty waters
Work their incessant and rhythmic magic,
Witness to generations of human experience
Of love and lust, births, marriages and deaths - of industry
In all its forms; of plagues and fire, of war and peace -
Of violence and crimes and the full panoply of man's
Mess upon this planet - and you remain the same.
Ever knowing, ever flowing - beautiful - serene.
When I survey your ebony depths - I also see reflected - London -
Perhaps an imperfect sum of man's noblest endeavours -
But still - lovable in its imperfection,
And ever hauntingly compelling.

Jane Finestone

BELMONT ROAD, UXBRIDGE

Wheels of shopping trolleys turn
        Where once the steam trains ran.
        The station's slipped downhill:
Transferring furrow-browed commuters,
Bringing happy shopping-seekers.

Yet still the Quakers, in their silence,
        Breathe a blessing
        As we pass.
What dear respite is their garden . . .
Mirrored in a tower of glass.

Pinafored girls not long stand
        By Victorian villas.
        Flowers in hand.
Where mothers clung to soldiers bright
Fearing for their earthly fight.

But naught has changed the uphill slog.
        Shopping laden.
        High-heeled shod.
O gentle gradient, how you hide
The thrashing to my heart inside.

Suddenly, a floral greeting!
        It lifts my weary spirit's
        Fleeting.
Golden roses hug the school,
Kept in check by gardener's rule.

At the top.
        Houses trim:
        All walled round with secrets in.
No shops. No trains. But laundry breeze
To blow the creases from our ease.

Kathleen McGuinness

SENSUOUS GOLDERS HILL

Gas light blues and whites
Splatter Golders Hill;
I feel their kisses on my cheek
And shudder at the thrill.

Regimented tulips
Marching to the band;
No luscious kiss from them,
Just a shaking of the hand.

Ikea-yellow daffodils
Searching for romances;
They softly hold my hand
And give alluring glances.

Fox gloves pink and pouting
Gently brush my knee;
They flutter at my side
And act suggestively.

Roses throw a sultry smile
Water lilies simper;
Iris slinky round my legs
Rejected pansies whimper.

Gladioli strutting
Luminous in the dark;
Nature caressing human life
Sensuous in the park.

Peter Phillips

THE WOMAN AND THE DOG

Underground she held him by a scarf,
tied to another round his neck.
In the street she stoops to loosen him,
leaves the second silk for ornament.

Visiting the daylight from the dark,
aloof, she strides down Piccadilly;
separate, she never spills a glance
to where he zigzags on the pavement,
doubling back to sniff a rubbish bin.

She never calls to him or whistles,
shows no nervousness even when
he hurtles at a kerb. He stops -
her total trust controlling him.

They disappear towards the dusk.

Virginia Rounding

WITHOUT YOU

Without you my life would be so bleak,
I need you near me week by week,
You are the stars up in the sky,
That always shine and never die.

Days may come, days may go,
The love I have I've got to show,
You are there I am here,
Come to me I need you near.

Sheila Osborne

LONDON'S LONELY

Hunched on a seat this figure of a man
seemingly lost, alone, withdrawn
behind that middle-distance look
stamped by self pity, anger and dispair.
Not only stark, but also bleak,
the message in this hollowed stare:
'Don't look, don't speak, I'm not here.'

All around rush-hour peak,
thundering trains and shuffling feet;
Every one a hurried fare . . .
this single figure isn't there.
He's not the city cardboard type,
more a bunkered bedsit kind
locked inside four shrinking walls
of a lonely, burnt-out mind.

'Drowning, not waving!' is the phrase.
Wave after wave of blanket faces
washes over London places;
Preoccupied and unconcerned
we live in *market-forces* days;
So-called progress, greater wealth . . .
but we don't see and have not learned!

Harold Rossney

KENSINGTON GARDENS - AUGUST 1965

Everywhere in the park
people are walking;
Under the great trees
people are talking,
By the Round Pond a
breeze is blowing.
High in the air the -
Kites are going.
In the deck chairs
people are sitting -
People reading,
People knitting.
Children laughing,
running leaping
Nannies nodding
Grannies sleeping,
And all the while
beyond these gates
Tumultuous swinging
London waits.

Isobel M Malcolm

GOOD MORNING SUTTON

Confetti petals flutter noiselessly to littered streets,
And scatter under chugging cars,
Spluttering damply to life.
Strutting pigeons peck hopefully at yesterday's trash
Dodging the early morning traffic, boldly.
Crumpled people crawl sleepily from night-warm beds
And curse the job they wish they'd never had.
Reluctant pupils drag on drab uniforms,
Trying to eradicate ingrained ink stains,
Hunting for homework, still unfinished.
Air hangs like wet washing, waiting for the sun.
Another day in Sutton has begun.

Penelope Guy

YELLOW BUSES

I hate these big monstrosities
That zoom around our town,
And most of all I do detest
The bilious bus of new renown.
Its shade of yellow, most precocious
A sickening colour, quite atrocious.

I'm a Londoner born and bred
London buses were always red,
It is a fact, like jellied eels
And Petticoat Lane and Bow Bell peals.
Away with buses sickly yellow
Bring back the well-loved crimson fellow.

G A Place

HEAVEN IN THE MAKING?

I live on London Road, Wallington, in a cosy flat
My home is shared with a crazy husband, and a tubby cat!
We have our own garden, which really is quite nice
(The cat uses it as stalking ground, and loves to bring in mice!).

Westcroft Leisure Centre is a short walk away.
Extensive facilities enables everyone to play
A selection of activities; try squash, tennis or swim
(Fancy pumping iron? . . Then try their high-tech gym!).

Visit Beddington Park if you prefer some peace and quiet
Lose weight walking miles and miles, there's no need to diet!
Alternatively feed the birds, or drink in *Henry's Table*
You could even row a boat if you think that you are able!

On the outskirts of this park, is Carew Manor School
Built in the 1400's, it's got a wonderful main hall
Orphans used to eat in this hall many years ago
And now it is a school where *special-needs* kids go.

Near Carew you'll see the graveyard and St Mary's Church
You'll find Sir Walter Raleigh's burial ground if you search
They say the School is haunted by his ghost, that's what I read,
And to cap it all the ghost is scaring folks without its head!

Wallington is convenient for bustling London city,
With an abundance of homeless people, it really is a pity
That folks don't spare them some coins to help them on their way
Still, I suppose some people really can't afford to pay?

The other side of London is shops, black cabs and nightclubs!
(Totally different from Wallington with burger bars and pubs)
If you like pickpockets, high speed police chases, and law breaking
Or shopping all day long, London is heaven in the making!

Janeyne Powell

ODE TO SUTTON

From Mitcham to Sutton we moved here one day
Eric works hard at Reed and Claire works hard at Hay
Half an hour from the station, the train takes her there
Eric just walks to work, lucky him there's no fare

A nice little flat in a nice little road
The humps? They're quite new, thank heaven traffic has slowed
The skips placed twice yearly we fill them so quick
The gritters come out when the snow falls too thick

Our stores are a pleasure in which we can shop
Mr Patel in the chemist for his help, in we pop
The two that sell papers come rain or come shine -
Outside Sutton station, they're now friends of mine

Sutton's famous mosaic is a picture to see
In St Nick's shopping centre is where you'll find me
Or the market twice weekly for fresh fruit and veg
I spend too much money - push hubby over the edge

The library that offers so much to each one
From music to history, it's serious, it's fun
It's a hive of activity for young and for old
But I'm sure we all use it to get out of the cold

So come on you all to a place that's just great
Everything you could hope for is here on a plate
On the outskirts of London, a town that's so dear
I bet you're now wishing that you could live here.

Claire Williams

THE LOST POND

Where's that pond?
That no one knows.
Secretly hidden,
Where, no one goes
To cast a gently fly.
The fish are big.
No fishermen need to lie.
Between the lilies is blue,
You mistake it for the sky.
The pond was lost
Many years ago.
In leafy wayside
The pond was hidden away,
From view, where oh! Where.
No body can say.
If you should seek to find.
That pond, that is lost
In the talk of time,
Ash your self is it real.
Or figment of some one mind.
Looking for something real.
A pond that's lost,
In myth of time.

Bryan Clarke

FIELD END ROAD

Field End Road is suburbia sprawling,
30's-type semi's and shops line the road.
The traffic is simply quite appalling,
There's little heed paid to the Highway Code!

The road through our windows presents each scene
Of daily life from dawn until midnight,
Dog-walkers and shoppers, some fat and some lean,
Mix with commuters in life's daily rite.

Drunks, after the pubs close, wend their way late,
Comic in efforts to stand all alone,
Not wanting the proffered arm of a mate,
Their songs vanishing into a distant drone.

Sometimes there is day-crime, thieves breaking in.
It happened to us - a most nasty surprise.
Neighbours both sides have suffered the same sin
By some petty crook, using his eyes.

Betterware reps, Avon and Kleeneeze,
They all come a-calling in Field End Road.
Whether it's calm or whether it's breezy,
They'll deliver the goods, load after load!

Window-cleaners also apply for trade,
They come once or twice, then oh, what a pain!
They all disappear from this leafy glade
Shinning their ladders in some other lane!

The semi's change hands, new neighbours move in,
Some shops close, others seem to survive well
They all form part of suburbia's din
And Field End Road's eternal pell-mell.

A Whitehead

LONDON TOWN?

Houses of Parliament,
Big Ben,
John (oh dear) Major at No.10.
Buckingham Palace,
Trafalgar Square,
On a Monopoly board we've all been there.
St Paul's Cathedral,
Oxford Street,
The River Thames where boats go to fleet.
Up to the Britts and,
Down to the pub,
Having a drink,
Watching Chelsea Football Club.
Eggs and bacon,
Pie and mash,
Everywhere else would think, they're trash.
So when it came to putting all this to the test,
There was no competition,
London is the best.

Tracy Francis (15)

BELOVED CITY

London, I love you still,
Despite the blotch, the patch, the greasy stain,
Despite the stinking drain,
The fog, the rain;
I have seen all these things
And I have heard the shrill,
Sharp, ugly squeak of brakes,
And love you still.

London, I love you yet,
Despite the bomb, the blast, the crumbling wall,
Despite the thunder-fall
Of stone and all;
I have known all these things
And I have heard the fret
Of sirens in the night,
And love you yet.

London, I love you more,
Despite the shops, the theatres where we met,
The pang of sharp regret,
The tears still wet;
I have known all these things
And I have heard the sore
Cry of a broken heart -
And love you more.

Brenda Hargreaves

KALEIDOSCOPE

Life begins at Hounslow - from the moment you arrive,
you can feel its vibrant pulses, the strong will to survive!
Just stop, look and listen - sounds and colours will stand out.
Market stalls - shops full of wares, children shouting about.
The mighty jets roar overhead, arriving from far and wide,
a panoramic kaleidoscope greets visitors inside.
The High Street beams a welcome from the neon signs below -
Not far away a baby is born - life begins at Hounslow!

Pearl Leeds

TO THE RISING SUN LAKE

Beneath a canopy of fluttering leaves,
Stirring gently in a summer's breeze,
With sunlight shafting through a verdant roof
We walked through paradise, a certain truth.

Accompanied by my two young sons,
On this day of rest, my week's work done,
We made our way towards our secret lake,
Walking quietly, for nature's sake.

I showed them the rounded home of thrush,
And brushed through reeds and spiky rush,
We spotted rabbit and squirrel and vole,
It pleased the eye and warmed the soul.

And in later years, when worldly cares
Cloud the brow, oft unawares,
Remembering those long ago days,
Lifts my heart and I am young again.

John Hibbert

SATURDAY MARKET

Where shall we go?
Why, Walthamstow!
Round the corner and
Down the tube
Nice bit of celery
Nice bit of food
This stall, that stall
There's bargains galore
Says Bet, 'Look at Katy.'
Says Katy, 'Look at that.'
A nice bit of 'at
Half a mile up and
Half a mile down
There's a nice bit of everything
there to be found.
Stop for coffee -
For Katy a fag,
Then a few more bargains
To fill up our bag.
Then back down the tube
onto the train,
Chatting and laughing till
We get home again
We had a good day
But we're glad to be back
With a nice bit of this
And a nice bit of that.

Katy Johnson

WINDY CHINGFORD!

That miserable wind is sighing over Chingford's parks and plains
Some trees are gaunt, some dying only bared twigs remain
The rain in torrents abounds and seals many a drainage cup
Flooding and warnings to prepare as we sand bag up

The wind is in a frolic over Chingford's parks and plains
It gathers up the decaying leaves and swirls them into chains
This blustering gale now giggles as we have to share and care
Concerned about our roofs and stacks a tiler's nightmare!

That wind is tormented jests haggles over Chingford's parks and plains
With bursts of renewed energy it battles to reclaim
The blast of all its anger is then heightened with delight
Continuing many frightful episodes well on into the night

Rubbish abounds caressed by the wind on Chingford's parks and plains
Plastic bags float like balloons as well as paper bags
Chaos with disposable cups and cartons litter the ground
The wind in it merriment has scattered all around

Settled now and contented is this wind that quietly blows
Over Chingford's parks and plains softly and tenderly goes
It seems so sad and has relented observing the damage that has been done
As secretly and smoothly, it escapes but it was fun

Those trees once dead are now in leaf soon flowers will appear
The wind is lulled back from its rest as it seeks solitude here
Once playing havoc and disturbing all is now serene
The parks and plains of Chingford wear now nature's mantel of green

R D Hiscoke

HIGH ON PARLIAMENT HILL

The sun was a kite
high on Parliament Hill the day
we walked tracing our hymn of joy
on the white icing. Charcoal branches
sprouted here and there lending painterly
contrast to the field in which we
bemused, caught clusters of people,
small, visually manageable, on skis
on feet on sleds in the distance
on the bridge over the iced pond just
looking . . .
'Sunday People Playing in Snow', a Dutch
landscape, Breughel composing
a number of available sports
and occupations the message simple:
people are colourful, people make warm
blobs, reds, greens, yellows, blues on white/grey
canvas. Perhaps it is also the other
way around. I pressed the gloved
hand of my companion, the one
outside the frame

Agnes Stein

HAREFIELD - CHURCH HILL IN THE SPRING

An ancient oak shades Church Hill's verge
The road climbs up towards the Green
And sturdy stands the Norman church
Amidst the yew tree's darkling sheen.
The common dressed in scabious bright
Attracts the butterflies' soft flight.

Almshouses crouch with latticed panes
Their red brick chimneys gaunt and high
And roses twine the picket fence
While rooks soar flapping to the sky.
And in the bushes sparrows peek
To fill each baby's gaping beak.

The King's Arms inn is by the Green
Where archers practised with the bow
In far-off days, and on the pond
The mallards dither to and fro.
And in the street the women stand
To gossip, baskets in their hand.

I pass the church where bells ring out
Where bridesmaids pose with dainty grace
Flowers glowing in their neat gloved hands
And mothers fuss with tearful face.
Church Hill has beauty in the spring
When cuckoos call and larks take wing.

Susan Coldwell

GRANPA'S CAP

My Granpa for himself at last
A winter's cap has bought.
For often did his head get wet
When in the rain was caught.
And when the freezing wind did blow
It wasn't very nice,
For then his poor old baldy head
Became a sheet of ice.
And birds would come from miles around
It was a sorry state.
To see them queuing up in line
To have a little skate.
Now Granpa likes his jolly cap
And this is what he said,
'I'll wear it in the bath sometimes
And always when in bed.'
My Granpa let me try it on
And it was plain to see
Though looking not too bad on him
It really suited me.

G Traveller

CAPITAL CITY OF GREAT BRITAIN

There she sits in regal splendour,
face uplifted to the sky.
With her steeples, domes and buildings,
flats that tower, up so high.

There are also statues, columns,
bridges, the people are passing by.
I often wonder, if they see,
the beauty that before them lies.

The parks in London are quite amazing,
laid out with such exquisite skill.
Yet look closely, nature's handwork,
and she's working on them still

What do you see when you visit London?
Do you see into the heart?
I think the thing, I see in London,
is living, breathing work of art.

J Dimmer

LONDON

In days gone by, when times were bad,
We made do with what we had.
Hand me downs and bread and jam
No such luxury as a *piece of ham*.
Old lamp lighters and the Muffin Man,
Our milk was measured in a little tin can,
Long hours I worked to reach my goal,
To buy some shoes without a hole.
But through it all, with no cash to spare,
I'm just glad that I was there,
In Dear *Old London Town*.

Joan Yeadon

BETWEEN TIMES

Memories of London, in the winter and the dark,
Serene in early morning, no traffic yet at play!
As Christmas decorations blazed out to light the way.
Down Kensington Church Street my favourite chandelier
Hung in a window; illuminated, bright,
A beautiful twisting spiral of iridescent light.
While on The Pond, in the nearby Gardens,
Out in the raw, blue, biting cold,
Sometimes there were happy skaters, skilled and bold.

Memories of London. Black cat who came by car,
Bringing a bag, food packed inside for him.
Why cafés would not let him in
He could not understand.
With table manners better than most,
He loved baked beans on toast
And a saucer full of milk.
It was different up in London, down Streatham way
He could either sit at table, or have a take-away!

Memories of London, alone in Hyde Park,
Watching spring sunrise start the day,
As bright yellow daffodils danced to sway
A greeting for so elegant Park Lane.
Busy mother duck, plus brood, a happy sight,
Crossed the road for breakfast, looking left then right!
Great horses out for exercise, while there was room to spare,
Monuments and palaces, grand squares and houses too,
Free from crowds of people, all for me to view.

London early morning, was the London that I knew.

Marion Green

INSPIRATION

Amid decaying concrete
brick and towering steel
new life stirs
inspiration for the
majestic sweeping curve
and line of architects
Every dawn a rising sun
embellishing man's fabrications
with lithe movement
powers nature's endless struggle
splashes of living green
reclaiming the endless brown
and grey modernity
within the debris of construction
this delicate life
a fragile totem for regeneration
for us
for our city

Jo Lee

UNTITLED

I've not lived long in Green Wrythe Lane
But I like it and think I will stay
There's a nice green field at the back, with views of afar.
I can see Ikea towers, oh what it inspires
especially at night in the dark. Oh-la-la.
Its circle of lights round the top of its rims
reminds me, of fairy rings.

Candice Armitage

TRANQUILLITY

A peaceful mind is a beautiful thing
No troubles on your mind at all
As peaceful as taking to the sky with a wing
You hear Heaven, for you call

Out in the heart of the country
Looking at the blue sky above
Peace and solitude you feel and see
And your heart's overflowing with love

When you have God walking beside you
You have His love and strength as well as your own
You can rest your body and more important your mind too
For God will take care of your worries and strife alone

In the country the nice slow pace of life, is great you feel
People are more friendly and have more time for each other
The lakes and rivers lie calm and still
It makes you care for the whole world as your own sister and brother.

Lynda Treacher

LONDON LIFE

London life
Never still or silent.
Day and night,
Always bold and vibrant.
A qualage of cultures,
Blue or grey.
London life
Takes your breath away.

T A Tinling

LONDON

London's a fabulous city
With all that is richest and rare,
But how will it help the old woman
Who stands on the pavement, there.

London has mansions and houses
And all that is finest and fair,
But how will it help the teenage girl
Who sits on the pavement, there.

The city abounds with hotels
And plenty of bedding to spare,
But how will it help the tired old man
Who lies on the pavement, there.

Restaurants are all around us.
We've eaten more than our share,
But how will it help the hungry young man
Who waits on the pavement, there.

London can offer all things
To those who have money to spare,
But what can it offer the person
Who dies on the pavement, there.

Jean English

LOVE AMONG THE RUINS OF LONDON
(Written during The Blitz)

In the desolated alleys near St Paul's
Dust still falls,
And by Paternoster Row, the bookman's haunt,
Ruins gaunt
Stand uncovered, as though mourning Fleet Street's pride -
Lost Saint Bride.

But in city wastes are churches once concealed,
Now revealed -
All the squalid blocks that hid their ancient stone
Overthrown -
And the quiet benediction of a sunset fires
Wounded spires.

Pricking up between the paving, shoots of green
Now are seen,
In a sheltered niche a bird finds spartan rest
For her nest -
There is love among the ruins; after strife
There is life.

Muriel Grainger

THINK CINQUE

Beyond Bickley and Bromley, lies country:
Neat hills, all elm tree crowned,
Dot the County of Kent - country of plenty!
Cropped grass, where sheep abound.
High hedges, that tunnel a funnel
Of green, where roads are clean,
From Oast Houses to *Leed's Castle* . .
Ride here - walk there; windmills lean
On the southern air. Peacocks strut
Near Tenterden. (Wide white Tenderden).
The beautiful Weald, cuddles and cossets
From thatch to swans, from forge to inn -
Near Tenterden! Then there is Rye:
Perched up high, *on guard* to the sky . .

Sylvia Ward

CARSHALTON PONDS

How proud the church
that overlooks the ponds
seems.
Such stately splendour,
A silent wide-eyed witness.
Some events would doubtless render
disbelief.
Circus elephants wading,
bathing their toes in
cool water.
Such rare behaviour.
Large, slow, exotic giants.
This small comfort was their saviour,
I believe.

Cheryl Morgan

SUTTON SERENADE

A cottage in Devon or Florida sun
Is by-passed by us now retirement has come
The sky of suburbia's as fleecy and blue
As any that brighten the post card view.

Though we don't have a cockerel to wake us at dawn,
The pigeons are cooing from trees round the lawn.
Nonsuch Park stretches green beneath rare-shapen trees;
Headley Heath's a short drive; birches bracken and breeze.

The library's the envy of less favoured places -
Café chat; study silence - and always as basis
Computers and head-phones and staff who like challenge,
With U3A too, to add spice to the mélange.

Neighbours are close friends or not, as we wish;
We network by interests; no small pond of fish
Do we swim in; but Westcroft's warm pool,
Where befriending's the option and not the rule.

A millennium of artefacts, painting and building
Bring trans-world tourists - cameras wielding
To the music and theatre and shops which are London
We can travel pass there and be back by sun-down.

Our children find work here; could call in each day;
Neither they, nor we, agonise, 'Are they OK?'
Nor need we stay long in our children's home
Where bed-times are later and TV's a groan!

There are, of course snags - concrete, traffic and thieves
But Florida too will suffer from these.
Picked companions, choice pursuits and family support,
Make living in Sutton too good to desert.

Anne Healey

ECHOES OF THE PAST

Echoes of the past.
Dreams of summer long.
Memories that last.
Long after evensong.

Dreaming of bygone days.
Of playing in the park.
Children's laughter lingers on.
Way on after dark.

Boisterous boys, fairground noise.
Boating on the lake.
Roundabouts, and hand me outs.
My grandma baked a cake.

Tra, La, La, Tra, La, La,
Gaily plays the band.
Little girls sang, while ladies danced.
And I held daddy's hand.

Echoes of the past.
Now summers nearly gone
Dreams are fading fast
Through the winter long.

Dreaming of bygone days.
Oh! Wasn't life just grand.
All this and ice-cream too.
On England's pleasant land.

Maggie Knight

DAGENHAM

Crown Street and Church Elm Lane.
A sloping village street.
Where I would walk to infant school,
With laggard scraping feet.

The country church where I was blessed,
The Cross Keys pub, nearby.
The windmill on corn chandeler's shop,
I see in memory's eye.

Crown Street and Church Elm Lane,
But now, no village street.
Another sacrificial lamb,
To lay at *planners* feet.

But, yesterday's nostalgia,
And I must leave it so.
Who am I, to prefer the sight,
Of the place I used to know.

Frederick Manning

SUNDAY SUMMER AFTERNOON

The backdrop is a blackbird's song.
Jets rush across regularly,
Still high enough above.
Rapping barbecuing beats -
At low-blast for all the family -
Hint of bit-part words and tunes:
Birdsong of its own.
Much closer to home,
My ears almost pop
With a high-pressure hush
Of car alarms in waiting.

Christopher Cuninghame

A POEM ABOUT LONDON LIFE

I need someone to hear me out
And listen when I wonder
The homeless are left
To struggle in pain
I thought all people were the same,
Soho pubs, strawberries and cream
Headlights flash their beams
In semi-darkened doorways,
The people in rooms above
Loud with endless chatter,
Placards with their enticing mottoes
Skyscrapers overhead
Down below a twelve year old
High on amphetamines.

Margaret Irwin

UNTITLED

Over the years the change has been thorough,
So let's all start to enjoy our borough,
Start with the library tap its great brain,
And you will come back again and again,
There's Times Square all polished and clean,
Always something fresh to be seen,
The shops here give off a glow,
It seems they are saying we know you know,
St Nicholas Centre another great treat,
This is really big the length of a street,
You can buy anything here,
Make sure you soak up the atmosphere,
There are at least fifty places for you to see,
No need to be fed up get out and feel free,
The London Borough of Sutton I'm proud to say,
We are new, we clean, and we are here to stay.

Marina MacLead

CAMDEN LOCK

Camden Lock was quite a shock, young people everywhere
Some were sitting on the bridge having braids put in their hair
A man in a car asked for money, while another played a guitar
And a girl with a rat on her shoulder called to the man in the car
His speakers thumped a beat out that was echoed all around
From shops and stalls all selling their wares which throbbed with sound.

The smells were indescribable as they wafted on the air
Incense mixed with curry and fresh coffee fused with beer
A man, his eyes not seeing, lifted his voice in song
While anothers not afflicted were intent on joining the throng
Who were sunning themselves by the water, earrings glinting from
                                                                               nose and from lips
While drinking their cans of lager, in big gulps no nice little sips.

Black seemed the favourite shade for most of their attire
With hair a riot of colour, some rivalling many a church spire
Now a young man rifles a rubbish bin, seemingly looking for food
And a girl yells abuse at her boyfriend, who answers with something
                                                                                    quite crude.

I wonder what the tourists think of this mad melee
Does this represent to them our Britain of today
Or will they see the wider scene, our history and tradition
Is this Camden Lock scenario just part of future vision.

P Hopkins

LONDON BOROUGH OF SUTTON

Back in 1933
My father, my mother, my brother and me
Came to Sutton from far off Wales
Leaving behind the mountains and vales
Sutton was one of the nicest towns
With one end leading to Belmont Downs

The other end led to a lovely green.
Nicely kept and very clean.
Quite nearby was a circular pond
Of which the children were rather fond
Mainly because it formed a riddle
Of how to get to the trees in the middle

The high street too was very fine,
With shops each side in one long line,
It boasted three large pubs as well
The Grapes, The Greyhound and *The Cock Hotel*
Still to be seen was the baker man
Sitting up straight on his horse-drawn van.

Trams were running to and fro
What a pity they had to go
Lots of the houses were very grand
They all stood where flats now stand
The Manor Park Library was big and bright
It looked so cheerie lit up at night

The houses, the manor, the public hall,
Have all passed on beyond recall
But Sutton is still a fine old place
Leaving just a little trace
Of Sutton as it used to be
Back in 1933

P Howarth

NEW THOUGHTS ON OLD LINES

Come, fairy godmother! Bring your magic flair
To where decay and suffering abound,
You'll see commuters slouch in deep despair
While hassled both above and underground.

Appear! And give your secret sign
To Finchley, Clapham and Highgate dwellers -
In fact, all who live near the Northern Line,
For we're London Transport's *Cinderellas*.

With your all-powerful wand you could double the staff,
They'd be clean-suited, fresh-faced and cheery,
Greeting us all with a smile and a laugh,
Eagerly helping and answering each query.

Please revitalise that mournful depressant,
Bring movement and light to enhance and enthral,
Transform the ghostly Mornington Crescent
With bustle to equal Prince Charming's ball!

Remove the reason for our covetousness
Of well-wheeled sisters like the Jubilee,
Whose water-tight carriages, new-built to impress,
Have immaculate floors and upholstery.

You could render our journeys clean, swift and dry,
If ever you came to put on a show.
But these thoughts are all just *pie-in-the-sky*,
For we know we're stuck with the status quo.

Because fairy godmothers and rags to riches
Are purely the stuff of pantomime,
So we'll stoically bear the shortcomings and hitches
Of the tattered, penniless, Northern Line.

June Armstrong-Wright

CAMDEN TOWN

There is a song
In the sour streets
In razored bottles
And the torn skin
Of brakes
Gone round the bend.

The cracked woman
Holds herself together
On one note
Of abuse.
Her neighbours nightly
Beat walls
Into mirrors.

The widower's *Epilogue*
*S*ings its Closing Signal
Through rows of wallpaper.
Windows snare open.
Headless
Curses wake bricks and mortar.
Mouths flex behind netting.

Sirens like grotesque cuckoos
Fade to Hampstead
While in our local a drunk
Is given a smile
From ear to ear.

Unleashed
Alsatians bark in back gardens
And owls, owls
Tawny lion-cubs with torch eyes
Tear the night
Searching for cadaver.

Tomorrow the social worker
The rent officer
The estate manager
Will shrug off
Ripe discords

Tonight there is song in the streets.

George Tardios

BEDDINGTON ... MY HOME

Sunrise over the darkened park
Warming the chilled autumn air
Gentle breezes kissing frosted leaves
As they descend to the hardened ground

Early activity can be seen through the haze
Walking dogs with hot steamy breath
Leaving trails in the cold dewy grass
As they head for distant lit homes.

In the silence of the dawning day
The River Wandle flows gently on
Winding through the sleepy village
Carrying secrets to its journey's end.

As I witness Beddington's opening eyes
I know I belong . . . I belong
Here is my refuge, my escape from the crowd
Here is my shelter, my home.

Sue Brotherwood

THE DIVISIONS ARE FINE

10am on a New York subway
A dim and distant memory, but just today
It was 10am on the Northern Line
Separate them at your peril, the divisions are fine

It was the same delays and hassle and hurry
The same foul odours from last night's curry
The same dead faces getting on the train
The same old hopelessness, I feel constrained
But it was in this country that I choose to stay
The United States of the UK.

Z100 blasts on Tottenham Court Road
See the crime and grime I fall in a pothole
As I walk past the homelessness and poverty
I go home to corporate sponsorship on ITV
With all these similarities, why did I move away?
To the United States of the UK.

A shopping centre is now called a mall
Pretty soon autumn will be renamed fall
The standards get lower, the accents are weaker
As the city gets familiar, the outlook gets bleaker
This is home sweet home, until my dying day
The United States of the UK.
God save the President, hip hip hooray!

Rona Topaz

BREAKING POINT

Smell car fumes
In the air we breathe, dust looms . . .
Empty promises of an economy set to bloom . .
Hope, a better life will come soon . .
Times are harder than they've ever been . .
I can't believe what I've seen people hungry, no food to eat . .
No money, crime rises . . so does the heat . . I've got to get some
                                        new shoes on my feet
Defeat stares the Londoner in the face.
What hath come of this great place, homelessness, jobs, issues
                                                to be debated,
Everyday at the House of Commons, the poor sit at home waiting
                                                to be evicted . . .
Who will deliver when all we do is take, for the love of the children . . .
                                                don't let this city break.

Ojeh

LONDON LIFE

London life is the life for me
Although it's not always filled with glee
Bar the selfish mode that Londoners are in
As they snarl in the traffic or swallow the gin!
It can be beautiful watching landscapes from bridges
Or a birds eye view of people and images
It can be educational take a butchers at Brixton
Or downright hysterical like the buildings in Euston
Yes London life is the life for me
With the cosmopolitan flavour that seeps through the tea
There's a few things I'd change as I walk towards Parliament
And still more to keep and I have a good argument
Yes London life I'm glad you are famous
Long live the beauty or did I mean chaos!

Malachi Hall

SELF CONTAINED

I cannot live within myself
My walls are much too thin
And every time my thoughts break out
The world comes rushing in

I cannot live within myself
My senses I can't bear
For all I see or smell or touch
Turns round and leaves a tear

I cannot live within myself
So I must live without
Without emotion, heart or soul
To lock all feeling out

Then I can live within myself
And introspective be
And isolate and insulate
Until there is no me

M W Donaghue

THE THAMES

The ebb and swell hums rippled tones
To penetrate the city's ancient bones
Ghosts of bygone times hide at every turn
But still among the ashes something burns
Impassioned by infinity life redeems the sodden shore
Damp driftwood and silvered stone rest silently forged
Strong and mighty river surging through
Noble as nature intended as melting jewels
In reflections at light of day and twilight stars.

Linda Yantolo

HOME

Home is where the heart is,
So the saying goes.
Home is where the heart belongs,
A place for love to grow.

Home is where, the growing's done,
Home is where, life has begun.
Home is sanctuary,
Safe and sound.

Home is where, we live and learn,
Home is where we hope and yearn.
Many a tear we laugh, we cry,
But home, is always home,
As years go by.

A Edwards

LONDON PRIDE

In old London town pearly queens and kings
London Pride, they used to sing.
If only they knew what time would bring.
Homeless people, beggars galore
Camp out for the night in each shop door.
'Spare any change' their mouths do utter
Looking for coppers in a rain filled gutter!
London pride? No, London shame!
To the politicians it's just a game
They don't care, it's getting worse
Don't wanna spend money from the Government purse.
So let's remember our forgotten
And make life for them a lot less rotten!

Carol Godfrey

LONDON IMPRESSIONS

London,
A very old island in an island,
an ancient white elephant
filthy through decay and neglect,
still holding its magic power.
The old stone lion
keeps its enigmatic smile,
as I walk through the drizzle.
On the mysterious river
boats, corpses, swans,
even flowers float . . .
A monster roars underground,
the tired travellers read evening papers:
'Young man killed by a wasp in park'.
London parks can be dangerous!
In an abandoned garden
there was a tree children used to climb,
they called it *The Elephant*
because of a trunk-shaped branch.
Now homeless kids sleep in boxes.
Under the trunk, a broken branch,
they chase the dragon. The void howls.
A bag-lady strokes a stray cat.
I share my stale bread
with some wild birds.
The grey clouds blow past the roofs,
towards the sea, close, far away.

London of a thousand worlds,
London of a thousand tongues,
surrounded by water, grass, muck, blood.

Antoinette Marshall

RANDOM SELECTION

So you live in London, what a scream.
A mix of nightmare and of dream.
A yummy ice cream in Regent's Park.
Footsteps behind you in the dark.
A man on his bike with mud up his back.
A girl in a pub dressed in leather all black.
A child in a shop, lost full of fear.
Sprayed on walls *are you queer?*

So you live in London, what a pain.
Constantly playing the promotion game.
Wait for the bus that never comes.
Kids with ulcers on their gums.
Long legs, short skirt but an ugly face.
She shouldn't be out in a decent place.
Throwing up on the Northern Line,
A mix of beer and Chianti wine.

So you live in London, oh what fun.
Carnaby Street in the summer sun.
Speaker's corner on Sunday morn.
They yell out. We laugh and yawn.
Camden Market blows my mind.
Niks and naks of every kind.
I love London, she loves me.
I am the fruit of the concrete tree.

John Manley

THE STREET WHERE I LIVE

I feel very strongly about my street
To me it holds no mystery
I've resided here for so long now
I'm quite conversant with its history

Litter here and litter there
My street is treated so unfair
Looking back I can say for sure
Took pride of place before the war

The cause is thoughtless humans
Who drop litter on their way
Drink cans, wrappers and papers
Discarded each and every day

The council is not blameless
There is far too much neglect
High taxes that we pay them
Should give streets much more respect

Everyone should make more effort
So that all our streets are clean
Then each would tread a neater path
Far more tidier than now seen.

Leonard E Tweed

LONDON

London isn't really
        a safe place to be
Not for the likes of you
        not for the likes of me

People are getting mugged
        each and every day
Sometimes they get caught
        sometimes put away

There is so much violence
        there is so much crime
It isn't safe to walk the streets
        after a certain time

But on the brighter side
        there's theatres and there's shows
Always places nice to eat
        and somewhere to go

If the crime wave fell
        and we could get the homeless off the streets
If there were more jobs around
        it would be a hard place to beat

Janet Larkin

LONDON TOWN

I was born in London Town
And proud I am to be
Part of dear old London
With its ancient history

Through the wars she did survive
Though parts were blown away
Still my London will remain
The place for me to stay

It's full of old traditions
And lovely buildings too
With dear old Father Thames
And Nelson high to view

The House of Lords and Parliament
Big Ben will chime the hour
And Number Ten Downing Street
Where Churchill dwelt with power

St. James's Park and the Mall
Westminster and The Strand
Hyde Park with all the speakers
And the old Salvation Band

Piccadilly and Leicester Square
Trafalgar Square with fountains
The lions sitting still and quiet
As if they were on mountains

The Changing of the Guards
All tourists love to see
Outside Buckingham Palace
They protect our Royalty

This poem is for England
And forever I shall be
Part of dear old London
With its ancient history

Enid M Roberts

SYDENHAM HILL WOODS

Sydenham Woods Saved.
The local paper says.
But this is not the first time,
The woods have been under threat.

The Governors of Dulwich College,
Have other plans for the woods.
It would be so much nicer,
If the woods could be replaced.

They'd like to build elegant houses,
With garage and beautiful views.
They'd have very exclusive tenants,
Affordable by only the few.

Southwark Council do not agree
They came down on the side of the trees,
But the Governors of Dulwich College,
Will be plotting again.

Margaret Jackman

CLOUDS OVER LONDON

After the promiscuity of summer
Passing through open windows
Into each other's homes
Barely dressed
The midday heat falling in slabs
September brings sanity
And clouds over London.
We can slope off into pockets
Of privacy.

The roads are almost deserted
At ten o'clock.
No stir of wind
Or passage of time.
Everything is at a distance
The shunting of trains
Marshalling
Of children in playgrounds.

John Rule

TWISTING OLIVER TWIST

Rejected by his mother's arms
Abandoned with, or without qualms
Rescued from the gutter's charms,
To a shelter, financed by alms

Oliver raised the bowl in his palms
And voiced some new demands,
Unlike those present then, and before
The greedy beggar wanted more

Discontent with equal share
Admonished from the floor,
Was so put out,
He turned about
And headed for the door

He found himself on a London Street
Learning sleight of hand,
And later how to fall on his feet
When he met someone grand.

Made into something royal
He learned to avoid real toil
When a guardian loyal
Unearthed legacy spoil.

Excuse me if I desist
Feeling sorry for Oliver Twist,
But save it for others on Dickens' list
Those trapped in poverty's grist
Grinding hungers cold hard fist;
And no better offer to resist

R Green

BY TRAIN TO EAST DULWICH STATION, LONDON

On my way to work in the train
I read my book
Or surreptitiously study the passengers,
Eaves dropping.

More often
I gaze out of the window
At short-lived panoramas:
People's back gardens,
High enclosing banks
With tall thin tree trunks
Like straight standing soldiers,
Then out over shiny slate roofs
And an irregular army of chimney pots.

I emerge onto the high platform
And plunge down the station path,
Surrounded by overarching bushes,
Bright berry laden branches,
Dark glossy-leafed shrubs
And the odd piece of coyly peeping rubbish.
Pervading all is the smell of damply rotting leaves.

As I turn out onto the pavement
Into the urban traffic,
I have a small sense of bereavement,
The sense of leaving behind
A secret hidden country
Which may not be there tomorrow.

Priscilla Noble

WHICH LIFE?

The huge fiery cannonball, known as sun,
Is sinking down slowly amongst a sea of colour,
The red brick of houses is blending in well,
And the windows are glinting, reflecting the sky.

An aeroplane crosses the fiery heavens,
It leaves a dissolving path.
A flock of starlings cross the plain,
Their cries faintly echoing.
A slight breeze blows, causing the trees to rustle.
Far away a horn sounds, startling a nearby school-girl,
She sighs at the ever-changing beauty,
Then carries on walking, to her warm love-filled home.

That same dramatic sunset, almost hidden from view,
Tries to peep through the solid, concrete buildings,
That tower high, and leave shadows big and forbidding.
The deserted streets are littered,
The rubbish-bins overturned by some hungry waif.

A motorbike zooms through the narrow alleyway,
Shattering any peace there was.
A stray dog comes around the corner,
A half-knawed bone in his jaw.
A dusty unwelcome breeze blows,
Somewhere in a gutter a foodwrapper flaps.
In the only shop doorway a homeless man sleeps,
He pulls his rags closer, to his limp, dirty self.
He is cold, unloved and helpless.

Isabel Tredinnick (11)

EBONY

My name is Ebony - hence my jet-black shiny coat
I wear a *posh* red leather collar around my throat.
I love my home - it's a little gem
Protects me from the world's mayhem,
I count my blessings every night,
By a glowing fire, a most comforting sight.
I'm not allowed to go out in the cold,
Pampered beyond belief - I am told!
Plenty of cuddles on my mistress's knee,
She tickles my tummy and I purr with glee.
The cat next door tells me how lucky I am
Being fed like a Lord on best chicken and ham.
All he gets told is - *out of the house*,
To catch his own dinner - a fat little mouse.
One thing's for certain, I'll never wander or roam,
From this life-style of luxury - I'm proud to call *Home*.

Nancy Shanks

ELBOWS GREASED

We live in London
We're at the centre
Don't take the mick
I'm sick
To see the life we lead
Up close
My nose smells dirt
The grime and crime
Of elbows greased and
ready to climb
Out of the pit
To mine the wealth
That's made
By London's grey ill health.

Andrew Nice

ON DOING RESEARCH INTO DONKEYS

The Borough historian likes the idea for sure.
All I can discover is about manure -
And the dust superintendent sacked for drink.
He signed the pledge, went over the brink.

Sad tale but here is seven Downshire Hill,
The house a history book would fill.
They sacked the man who did not call;
Saved - complainant could not identify at all.

On through the pallied sheets with their brown ink,
Tired eyes ever on the blink.
The family to be reduced by five,
Rest in basement room to thrive?

Not much on donkeys, though Gayton Road sold asses' milk.
Let's have more nuggets of that ilk;
And thank the Christian who made heartless shake
When he said donkeys for their lunch must break.

I'm stuck for now. To the Veterinary College,
        Please write in.
Perhaps the information there is not too thin

Joanna Mackay

CRYSTAL PALACE

A dozen venuses lie in disarray
All clutching cloth to protect their modesty,
Trapped behind an iron fence,
Still scattered from the great fire . . .
And Tubby Isaacs sells the best seafood in town

On this spot stood the Crystal Palace,
In which people stared up in wonder
At a world compacted into one hall
Until the flames set it free
And Tubby Isaacs sells the best seafood in town

This is where Utrillo painted and Monet . . . Pissarro,
Where Zola hid in exile after Dreyfuss
Now Kwiksave sets the prices to beat
Crystal Palace gets its air fresh from the sea
And Tubby Isaacs sells the best seafood in town

Martin Nathan

THE BRANCHES OF THE YEW TREE

There is a town called Yiewsley
Built in the lea of a yew
The roads all around are named after trees
Like the elm, the willow and poplar too
There's an ash, an acacia and an apple you see
The sycamore, the chestnut and laburnum on view
With the maple, the birch, the cedar and cherry
Not forgetting the whitethorn, lilac, and pear with the yew
But how did i get in Yewsley
I came down Fairway and across Lawn
Along Colham Green and into Station
Under the bridge and up high over the canal
How about you?
Or Yew!?

Keith Ayres

URBAN ZOO

Dirt gets sprayed on wet grey days,
from the river of metal outside my front door.
The windows tremble and get dirty again,
my family survive this environmental war.
Neighbours are quiet. I needn't ask why.
Victims of opinion? Or are they a bore?

But! It's springtime again,
A beautiful day, the birds sing and
'Hello, nice weather' welcomes my ears, don't rain
as this community of people smile for a change,
it's nice to walk down the lane.

As daylight comes once more to a close,
the shops dim their lights and shutters come down.
Kids hang around, bored I suppose,
kicking walls down and smashing windows.
The Cherry Tree pub locks out the night drinkers,
to whistle, laugh and shout all through the town.

As I lay down my weary head,
the last of those voices fade away.
Long haul lorries fill the air with lead,
meeting the needs of the busy airport.
I wake with a start, mornings appeared,
to greet the days workers out of their beds.

I shut the door of my humble abode,
and set out again just down the road.
Queues of people wait for the bus,
looking at watches and making a fuss.
For pregnant mothers seeds have been sown,
A new generation down Sipson Road.

Michael Austin

SWISS COTTAGE LIBRARY

Neat as a Japanese forest
the books are shelved
leaning to the townscape
of glass and brick
to be glimpsed through
the upright windows.

The sun, pale lemon
on a cold October day,
dies behind the cinema.

Sound hurries sound;
footsteps spiral
the wooden slats.
Pages turn and all pervasive
the electric hum
of the hidden lights.

Silence bandaged in sound,
swathed like a child;
eclogues for the first time read,
burgeoning music hidden
in the womb of silence;
another layer of sound.

Sound conceals sound,
silence, silence
until a vacant space
between fern and fish
stares in silent sight
when sound and silence are one.

C H Wood

KINGS CROSS

We are on parole from the safe
Custody of marriage, confined
Within the time-table of a suburban train.
Nothing dangerous will escape from this cafe.
Our conversations trawl the past
There are several missing years.

Are they stored somewhere the answers
To all the questions I have hoarded?
We started so many sentences
But the ends were lost in popular music.
My hand kept reaching for your neck.
Your shoulders were always hunched
Against the cold or your low expectations.
One night in Westbourne Grove
We played pool and your eyes spat fire.
There was no buffer between our emotions.
Words circled endlessly frightened
To land on anything less than the truth.

We say none of this, it goes on
Over your shoulder while you talk.
The sunlight bounces off the roofs of cars
Inching around Kings Cross.

John Gould

HAMPSTEAD HEATH

Ancient Heath
Encroached by putrefying
Furnaces,
Your little gift of
Rural England -
Seductive and untamely -
Reminds us of our
Fate in the hands of

Tertiary Industry;
Sedate money making.
Power for your cars and
Narcissistic selves.

Hundreds retreat there,
To the Heath
Seek out a secluded spot
Beneath the canopy.
Heads bob in the
Long grass
Like rounded sheep,
Lost in a wilderness.

Susan Crocker

LONDON

Stand in awe, you young or old,
For this is London, its streets paved with gold.
Here is history and culture from all around the world,
From days bygone, wherever Union Jacks wereunfurled.

Great palaces, stately homes, theatres and pubs,
And colourful shopping malls with trees in large tubs.
Well known restaurants, good places to eat,
A chance to refresh and to rest weary feet.

Statues, tall columns, museums, Roman relics too,
Art galleries, music halls, operas and ballet for you.
Buckingham Palace, Parliament, Big Ben, plus dungeons and moats,
Docklands, Tower Bridge, the Thames and river boats.

Crown Jewels and Beefeaters - Baker Street and Sherlock Holmes,
Artifacts of William Shakespeare to Carnaby Street, red boxes and phones.
Even architectural masterpieces from which travellers board trains,
And places of learning for those with keen brains.

Medical institutions, Westminster Abbey, New Scotland Yard and the Cutty Sark,
The Old Bailey, Kew Gardens and Marble Arch.
Climb aboard HMS Belfast and chat with the Skipper,
Then tour ancient streets once stalked by Jack the Ripper.

It has been said 'when one tires of London, one tires of life!'
A rare treat for the visitor at an affordable price.
'Yes', do make the journey, learn and explore,
Be assured, once you have seen it, you'll come back for more.

Harry Fenton

LONDON, A LIFE

London life from far away
my dreams call within.
Flashing lights and streets so bright,
I want to call and visit again.

Nineteen Eighties was the boom,
so I packed a bag, checked the tag
and flew on over, bypassing the moon.

I booked a room in Clapham, a bedsit for my needs.
To toss my load upon the bed,
when I arrived home greeted by fleas.
I got a job in London, where cranes were to the full,
working on the building site, where work was plentiful.

Good times were had by one and all,
money filled my pockets and the bank loved it too.
I never took a holiday for I worked, on through,
but looking back, I wish I had,
for the dream soon finished for me.

Jobs were going, sites were closing frequently.
The signs were going up on jobs, no labour required.
I should have taken notice then,
and skiddaddled back on home, over.

But I took my chances within my grasp,
thinking this will pass.
London is a life for me, as I ponder my next move,
not from room in Clapham, but from this cold damp underpass.
I'm fed by strangers now,
at the Holy Cross resort.
I thank and cherish the time I had, of ten years long past,
for now, London is for me, a life.

Martin Connolly

YIEWSLEY

I went for a walk this morning
Through the main high street in my town
It once was a thriving, clean centre
How Yiewsley has been *closed down*.

Shop after shop has been shuttered
For sale, to rent, to pull down.
Every where litter, dirt or graffiti
Yet this could be a proud town.

Open up shops for the people
So we don't have to go further away.
Clean up the streets, bring out some paint
Making an effort would pay.

Let's put Yiewsley back on the map
Encourage all people to trade.
Let's have Marks, British Home Stores and Iceland
Let Yiewsley be shown *A1 Grade*.

Marion Pinder

UNTITLED

I would go down on bended knee
And take your hand in mine,
And say those words you want to hear,
As a husband, you'd be fine!

But if things didn't go as planned
I didn't serve you well,
You'd probably arrest me and
You'd put me in a cell!

It is the 29th Feb
That I know for sure,
But I don't think I will take the plunge
Not 1984.

Maybe 1988
If you're passing by
But I think I'll leave it for a while,
I'm really rather shy!

L D Mellish

THE LURE OF LONDON

It's 1995 as Big Ben chimes
The revellers are having a ball
London is alive and kicking
There's a welcome here for all.

They love dear old London
She's so bubbly and bright
Full of life by day
And sparkling by night.

From the rolling river Thames
To the outline of St Pauls
History reigns supreme
Within her city walls.

Statues, museums and theatres
Are part of her rich treasure
Together with verdant parks
They give us endless pleasure.

Taxis and buses amble along
Full of tourists from afar
This cosmopolitan capital
Knows no colour bar.

To see Marble Arch on a spring day
Cannot be surpassed
London has something for us all
Her beauty is regal and vast.

Margaret Robinson

FORGET-U-NOT

Don't ask me to remember
The days we shared at school -
The playing-field mist in November . . .
And Matron's gooseberry-fool . . .
It's not that I'm being cool
Or terribly set in my ways,
But I've made an absolute rule:
I won't remember those days!

You'd like me to be a member
Of the Old Boys Club at school?
Only twenty quid each December?
'Thanks, no', I must say *you tool!*
My other leg please pull.
Life's now in a different phase,
And though I may seem a mule,
I *won't* remember those days.

For you it was, in the swimming-pool,
With Harris and Wilson and Hayes,
Who tied me onto your ducking-stool -
No, I won't remember those days!

Adrian Vale

RIP THE SWEET CHESTNUT TREE OF WANSTONIA

A car was left on this street long ago
Now rusted solid it stands
See the flowers growing in the upholstery
Weedy flora; they should be lilies.

Before the police and builders came to stay,
We used to have muggings here every day.
Walk in Leyton after dark
There stands a street particularly stark.

Far from the city, in the forest, on the heath;
We walked with muddy tracks beneath
There was no sound from cab or bus
When the roads belonged to all of us.

Our felled trees are now never to be resowed
The mists of time are dust from a city road
The road to progress beside which a beggar squats, waiting
Surrounded by a concrete world's consolidating.

Progress progresses in progression
The sun rises, glints off of the machines and plastic helmets
Of the assembled workers.
In East London rose brick structures
For riders of the central line.

The city slums were burnt
The city slums were purged
The East End homes were demolished
Hackney dwellers will be routed
The red route of progress lays waste today.
Seven-foot walls guard the motorway.

Where once stood a residential street
The residents prepare to meet defeat.
A ruthless fate will be edicted
And Claremont Road will be evicted.

L E Wirtz

HAYES END ROMANCE

By nettle dock and bramble,
Between fields cow parsley white.
My thoughts would often ramble,
And I'd see you in a different light.

The leafy elms the ancient oak,
Entwine and tangle overhead.
The pathway of which we never spoke,
Where once I feared to tread.

I dare not cross that narrow line,
Between a lover and a friend.
Dark the knowledge you can never be mine,
Alone I walk to the end.

Fields of Middlesex still forgotten,
Developers kept at bay.
Fence and paling, overgrown and rotten,
I am surrounded by decay.

Behind me weaves the beaten track,
Ahead the future black as night.
Only you can lead me back,
To those fields cow parsley white.

In the mellow hush at days end,
Old flames are lit in vain.
A cold wind blows from Hayes End,
To put them out again.

Ron Lamerton

JUST UP MY STREET

Charming houses line the street,
pavements echo with scurrying feet
people smiling always pleasant,
welcome you to Wentworth Crescent!

Students dwell across the way,
no one knows how long they'll stay
perhaps they're German or are they Dutch?
writing home to keep in touch!

Well kept gardens, lush and green,
with hollyhocks that stand serene
neighbours stop and chat for hours,
about the plants and splendid flowers!

People waiting for their post,
watch for the postman, as they eat their toast!
will he bring a welcome letter
with news that's only for the better?

A mini-cab calls and has to wait,
for the working girl, who's always late
ever patient, always there,
while she decides which dress to wear!

So every house can tell a tale,
whether just moved in, or up for sale
now my poem appears complete,
it says it all, just up my street!

Jasmine H Newing

INFORMATION

We hope you have enjoyed reading this book - and that you will continue to enjoy it in the coming years.

If you like reading and writing poetry drop us a line, or give us a call, and we'll send you a free information pack.

Write to

        Arrival Press Information
        1-2 Wainman Road
        Woodston
        Peterborough
        PE2 7BU.